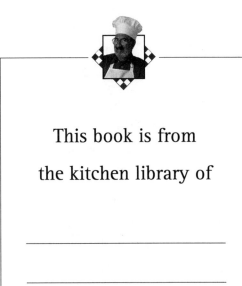

This book is from

the kitchen library of

_____

_____

ALSO BY ART GINSBURG, Mr. Food®

The **Mr. Food®** Cookbook, OOH IT'S SO GOOD!!™ (1990)

Mr. Food® Cooks Like Mama (1992)

Mr. Food® Cooks Chicken (1993)

Mr. Food® Cooks Pasta (1993)

Mr. Food® Makes Dessert (1993)

Mr. Food® Cooks Real American (1994)

Mr. Food®'s Favorite Cookies (1994)

Mr. Food®'s Quick and Easy Side Dishes (1995)

Mr. Food® Grills It All in a Snap (1995)

Mr. Food®'s Fun Kitchen Tips and Shortcuts (and Recipes, Too!) (1995)

Mr. Food®'s Old World Cooking Made Easy (1995)

"Help, **Mr. Food®**! Company's Coming!" (1995)

Mr. Food® Pizza 1-2-3 (1996)

Mr. Food® Meat Around the Table (1996)

Mr. Food® Simply Chocolate (1996)

Mr. Food® A Little Lighter (1996)

Mr. Food® From My Kitchen to Yours: Stories and Recipes from Home (1996)

Mr. Food® Easy Tex-Mex (1997)

Mr. Food® One Pot, One Meal (1997)

Mr. Food® Cool Cravings (1997)

Mr. Food®'s Simple Southern Favorites (1997)

Mr. Food®'s

Italian Kitchen

Art Ginsburg
Mr. Food®

WILLIAM MORROW AND COMPANY, INC.

NEW YORK

Library of Congress Cataloging-in-Publication Data

Ginsburg, Art.
    Mr. Food's Italian kitchen / Art Ginsburg.
        p.   cm.
    Includes index.
    ISBN 0-688-14396-2
    1. Cookery, Italian.   I. Title.
TX723.G479   1997
641.5945–dc21   97-19705
                                                                            CIP

Printed in the United States of America

First Edition

1 2 3 4 5 6 7 8 9 10

BOOK DESIGN BY MICHAEL MENDELSOHN OF MM DESIGN 2000, INC.

www.williammorrow.com

www.mrfood.com

Dedicated to

The influence of Troy's
Havermans Avenue and Hill Street
neighborhoods

Aah!! What wonderful memories I have of the
great tastes and aromas of
oh so many meals shared there!

Acknowledgments

When we think of Italian cooking, we think of the tastes and smells of home-cooked food made with love and the best ingredients . . . and there's usually *lots* of both! We also think of get-togethers with family and friends where we get to share good food and good times. Yup, that's what *I* think of. And Italian food automatically makes me think of the important people in my life, too, 'cause eating it is an experience—one that should be shared.

Howard Rosenthal helped me gather ideas and recipes and supervised all the food preparation, while my daughter, Caryl Ginsburg Fantel, helped me organize my thoughts and whipped everything into shape until it was done just right.

For this book I was fortunate enough to be surrounded with quite a few other people who're important to me. It all starts in the kitchen, and I thank my kitchen staff for being right there with me to toss the pasta, brown the veal, and layer the Tiramisù. There's Patty Rosenthal, who added her own TLC to each dish; Janice Bruce, with her attention to detail; Cheryl Gerber, who kept us smiling; Joan Wolff and her never-ending energy; and Karen Tandlich, who kept things humming along to her Italian tunes. Al Barron, our jack-of-all-trades, always had our supplies at hand, even before *we* knew what we needed! And Joe Peppi once again kept us all organized by orchestrating and documenting everything we did in the kitchen, while Laura Ratcliff entered recipe after yummy recipe into our computer.

Acknowledgments

Now, like I said, you can't have a feast without lots of people to share it with! My thanks to my wife, Ethel, for accompanying me on this terrific journey, to my son Steve for overseeing the day-to-day goings-on of our business, and my son Chuck for managing everything for our one hundred forty-plus TV stations. I appreciate the creative input of Helayne Rosenblum and Ruth Dickson. I thank Tom Palombo for his sales and licensing expertise, as well as our Controller, Chet Rosenbaum, who truly makes it all add up. My assistant, Marilyn Ruderman, keeps me organized on and off the road. And Alice Palombo, Carol Ginsburg, Beth Ives, and Heidi Triveri are my very special support team who hold down the fort.

Then there's my extended family: I love thanking my agent, Bill Adler; Bill Wright, President and CEO of the Hearst Book Group; Paul Fedorko, Senior Vice President and Publisher of William Morrow; Editor Zachary Schisgal; and Assistant Editor Anne Cole. Then there's the rest of the Morrow team, led by Richard Aquan, Deborah Weiss Geline, Lisa Dolin, Michael Murphy, and Jackie Deval. Of course, designer Michael Mendelsohn and illustrator Philip Scheuer really set the table well for this beautiful feast. Thanks, guys!

I owe special thanks to Michael Cocca, a dear family friend who shared so much of his own Italian heritage and knowledge of Italian food during the preparation of this book. His hints and tips were the next best thing to a personal tour of Italy for us all!

Once again, I wish to express my appreciation to my viewers and readers. My pasta pot is overflowing with thanks to all of you for encouraging me to keep on cooking.

Acknowledgments

The following companies were especially helpful in making this book possible, and I want to thank them for their consideration and generosity:

Badia Spices, Inc.

Krups, makers of quality blenders and mixers

Sargento Cheese Company, Inc.

Villa Valenti Classic Sauce Company

Contents

Introduction

Hi there, and welcome to my kitchen . . . or maybe I should say *"Buon giorno"* and welcome you to my *Italian* kitchen. Just look around and you'll see that my kitchen is full of all types of Italian favorites that'll have you begging for more and more. Oh, I hope you're hungry, 'cause there's lots to share and, yes, as with all my books, these recipes are all easy to prepare.

Wanna have your friends and family thinking you went to an Italian cooking school? Tell 'em how Italian celebrations have lots of different courses, each as important as the next, then dazzle 'em with a hot or cold antipasto. Why, you can even make a whole meal of a variety of dishes from the same course! Actually, *antipasto* means "before the meal," but you could serve a meal that's a variety of antipastos. You just might be convinced to do that after you see the chilled meal starters that I've got for you. From Marinated Garden Vegetables and Prosciutto and Melon Skewers to Deluxe Antipasto Platter, these taste as pretty as they look!

Feel like getting your meal started with something hot? Dig into one or a few hot antipastos. There's Stuffed Baby Eggplant, Vegetable Turnovers, and even Fontina Fondue. Just make sure you've got nice long skewers for dipping into *this* one!

When you're in the mood for a steaming bowl of hearty Italian soup, that's no problem. I've got the recipes for pot after pot of classics like Pasta e Fagiole, Lentil Soup, and Spicy Sausage and Bean Soup. Of course, I want you to feel free to start with my recipes, then go your own way with them, since every Italian cook has his or her own version of Pasta e Fagiole (pronounced by most Americans as "fah-zool") . . . and everything else!

And as long as we're making soup, what could be better than dipping into it with some fresh-baked bread and maybe enjoying it with some right-from-the-oven homemade pizza? Why, I've got a chapter brimming with breads and pizzas that you can make in no time. Sure! There's Spaghetti Sauce Bread—a basic Italian bread with a new twist—Sesame-Parmesan Bread Sticks, and a couple of versions of focaccia. Sounds tempting, right? These and the rest of the breads and pizzas promise to be so crisp and melty-good you won't know which one to make first!

Okay, the next course of our meal, called *primo*, is usually a big plate of pasta. Oh, there are so many types of pasta to choose from, not to mention the countless ways to make it. Why, I chose so many that I didn't have enough room in one chapter . . . so I made two! The first is full of toss-together pasta dishes that are done in minutes, like Mushroom-Broccoli Cavatelli. And how 'bout that Fresh Tomato Linguine? It's so tasty that it's sure to become part of your regular world cooking tour.

So, you *think* you have willpower. We'll see about that when my oven-baked pasta dishes and casseroles come bubbling out of the oven. Watch out—Angel Hair Pie, Broccoli and Cheese Manicotti, and Eggplant Parmigiana are almost impossible to resist. And those are just three of the seventeen baked favorites.

How could we have an Italian kitchen without lots of sauce? After all, the sauce is what flavors almost every pasta dish! And once you taste some of these goodies, like Roasted Red Pepper Sauce, White Garlic Sauce, and Classic Alfredo Sauce, you're gonna want to cook up pasta every night . . . and happily end your meal right there.

But you can't! Next we move on to the course called *secondo.* That's where our fish, chicken, and beef dishes come in. I've made sure we've got plenty of simple Italian-style recipes here, from the popular tastes of Quick Chicken Marsala and Prizewinning Lemon Chicken to fancier Cornish Hens in Chianti Sauce, Braciola (it's as Italian as they come), Braised Mediterranean Beef (so tender you can cut it with a fork), and Lemon Pork Tenderloin, a light and lemony change of pace.

Of course, if you're hooked on seafood, my kitchen has quite a selection for ways to make everything from fillets to steaks, with shells on and shells off. Oh, your mouth will be watering for those scallops in zesty oregano sauce and shrimp swimming in amaretto sauce. And there are good old Italian Fish Cakes that are just perfect for dunking in rich marinara sauce.

If you're not full yet, you're gonna love the choices in my rice and potato chapter. Just try to stay away from my risottos! I've got a few of them and they're so creamy, you're guaranteed to ask for seconds. (And, yes, risotto really is easy to make!) There are fluffy rice dishes (you'd better be prepared to make double batches!) and Special Roasted Potatoes that are, well, really special . . . you'll know exactly how they got their name!

Yes, in my Italian kitchen we all eat our five servings a day of fruit and veggies. It sure won't be a problem finding something to accompany your *secondo* dishes when you see the offerings in my vegetable chapter. With recipes for Sicilian Zucchini, Broccoli Rabe Sauté, and Vegetable Frittata, I know it won't be hard to get *you* to eat *your* veggies, either!

I don't know about you, but I'm getting pretty full . . . so full that I might only be able to have one *dolce* (dessert), or maybe half of two! (I always have a hard time choosing just one to make.) Should I choose Tiramusù, Rainbow Cookies, Italian Plum Tart, Lemon Ice, or Cannoli Pie? It's just not fair! And I know that once *you've* experienced and shared the tastes and aromas of my Italian kitchen, you'll have no choice but to join me in saying, *"Mamma mia,* I love all the 'OOH IT'S SO GOOD!!*'"*

Pasta Cookin'

Cookin' pasta is practically as easy as boiling water! Even though it's hard to mess it up, there are a few things you might want to know to help you make perfect pasta every time.

- Generally, cook pasta in a large pot of boiling salted water, allowing about 1 quart of water for every ¼ pound of pasta. (It's not necessary to add oil to the cooking water.)

- Slip the pasta into the boiling water a little at a time, so that the water keeps boiling. And stir immediately so the pasta doesn't stick together!

- Fresh pasta cooks quickly, usually in just 2 to 3 minutes; dried pasta takes between 7 and 12 minutes. Always check the specific package directions.

- Stir pasta occasionally, checking for doneness. Cook it just to desired doneness, then drain.

- I recommend rinsing pasta only when it's going to be used for a cold salad or when it isn't going to be used immediately.

How do you know when it's done? When it sticks to the wall! Don't believe me? It's true! One of the loads of different ways that people test their pasta for doneness is to toss a piece against the wall. If it sticks, it's done! Or, a more conservative method is the bite test. Oh, I know that some people like their pasta really soft and mushy, but most pasta lovers (and Italian cooks) cook it *al dente*, which literally means "to the tooth." That means the pasta's got a bit of slightly undercooked core, giving us something to chew! Besides, when you cook pasta too long, it absorbs so much cooking liquid that it can't absorb much (if any) sauce—and the finished dish ends up really watery. Also, if you're planning to cook the pasta further, say, in a dish like Baked Penne Primavera, Broccoli and Cheese Manicotti, or Baked Rigatoni, make sure the pasta is even a little firmer after boiling.

Know Your Olive Oil

If you take a look into any Italian kitchen, you're sure to find several types of olive oil. Why? All olive oils are not created equal! I'll explain why we need a variety.

Extra Virgin Olive Oil, recognizable by its greenish color, rich olive flavor, and fruity aroma, is the best olive oil for recipes served chilled or at room temperature and for adding to finished dishes. Oh, yes—extra virgin olive oil is also the priciest olive oil.

Virgin Olive Oil, with a mellower taste than extra virgin olive oil, is still quite flavorful, making it a popular choice for cooking, dressings, and serving with bread.

Olive Oil, often referred to as "pure olive oil," is usually a blend of virgin and refined olive oils. Although it's super in salads and cold foods, it's the olive oil most commonly used for sautéing, since it has the highest burning point.

Light Olive Oil, lighter in color and taste than the other varieties, is *not* lighter in calories. It *is* versatile, though, since it can be used when a less "olive-y" taste is desired.

Not only is olive oil a flavorful kitchen helper, but it contains no cholesterol! And now that I've told you about the different types, I'll tell you that you really need to keep only one or two types on hand—maybe a bottle of virgin olive oil for dressings, and a bottle of pure olive oil for cooking.

Stored in a cool, dark place, olive oil (all types) should last for up to 6 months from the time of purchase. It can be stored in the refrigerator for up to 1 year. However, storing it in the refrigerator will cloud the oil. But don't worry—it clears once it returns to room temperature.

When shopping for olive oil, don't be fooled by fancy labels and catchy package wording. The brands will vary, so why not buy a small bottle of any particular brand and try it out? You be the judge.

Say "Italian Cheese"

Say "Italian cooking" and we immediately think of foods like lasagna, pizza, and spaghetti and meatballs. One thing many Italian recipes have in common, besides being irresistible, is that they feature cheese. And boy, is there a variety of favorite Italian cheeses, from soft, spreadable ones to hard grating ones. Here's a quick list that should help you know which to use for what.

Asiago is a rich, nutty-flavored cheese made from cow's milk. Aged Asiago has a firm, hard texture and is ideal for grating and shredding. Asiago gets stronger with age, so younger Asiago is a bit mellower, making it a perfect snacking cheese.

Fontina is a mild semi-soft cheese typically aged for between 3 and 4 months. It's super sliced for sandwiches and for melting in a wide range of dishes.

Gorgonzola comes in two types—a younger, creamy, delicate-flavored variety, aged for about 3 months, also known as *dolce,* that's great for cooking because of its excellent melting quality. Firmer Gorgonzola, also referred to as *naturale,* is similar to our domestic blue cheese, but not usually as sharp. It's perfect for crumbling onto salads and pasta dishes.

Mascarpone is a soft, sweet Italian cheese, similar in consistency to soft cream cheese. It's commonly used in dips and in sweet dishes like Tiramisù.

Mozzarella is probably the most popular Italian cheese. The cured variety is the type most often used in the United States for topping pizza and baked pasta dishes. Made from cow's milk, it is widely available in varieties made from skim or part-skim milk. Its consistency makes it ideal for shredding, slicing, and chunking.

Fresh mozzarella, or, as they call it in Italy, *mozzarella di bufala,* is quite different. Traditionally made from buffalo milk, it's sometimes referred to in the United States as buffalo mozzarella. Fresh mozzarella is a very soft, mild white cheese that's enjoyed simply sliced and teamed with fresh tomatoes and basil, as in Fresh Mozzarella and Tomato Salad. It can be found in the deli department or specialty cheese section of larger supermarkets, often stored in water. Look for fresh mozzarella. It's worth the search.

Parmesan is a hard cheese that's most often seen grated. Its strong taste and aroma make it a perfect addition to many dishes. Aging gives Parmesan its rich flavor. Parmesan is relatively low in fat and, because of its intense flavor, a little goes a long way. You can buy it in chunks and grate it yourself, or choose one of the many varieties of shelf-stable grated Parmesan cheese; these generally contain anti-caking agents to reduce clumping.

Provolone is a firm cheese with a mild smoky flavor. Often found prepackaged in the dairy section, provolone is also available in the deli department for slicing as well as shredding. Longer-aged provolone has a sharp, almost spicy flavor.

Ricotta is a smooth, moist, creamy cheese similar to cottage cheese. American ricotta is usually made from whole or part-skim cow's milk, though its Italian counterpart was originally made from sheep's milk. Ricotta cheese is most often found in cooked items like lasagna and cheesecakes. Low-fat versions are commonly available these days.

Romano is a hard grating cheese, similar to Parmesan yet stronger-flavored. Romano is often sold already grated and mixed with Parmesan. Anti-caking agents are often added, along with salt, to increase shelf life.

Let's Talk Moderation

It used to be that when we thought of Italian cooking, we thought of pasta teamed with hearty meat sauces, bubbling casseroles topped with thick melted cheese, and rich, heavenly desserts. It was hardly what we would think of as "light" food . . . but that has changed!

Today we can use moderation with our Italian recipes to make them fit in with our lighter-style eating. I've got lots of ideas here that'll help you modify and "lighten up" most of the recipes in this book. For instance, you can cut down on both fat and calories quite a bit just by using nonstick pans and nonstick cooking spray. Simple enough? So are my other tips! So keep these handy as you cook. Of course, each of us has our own dietary requirements, so always consult your physician for your own specific guidelines. Then go ahead and make changes that'll work for you.

EGGS

In many cases, we can replace whole eggs with egg whites. (Two egg whites equal one whole egg.) And, yes, in most recipes, you can go ahead and replace eggs altogether with egg substitute. (It's usually available near the eggs in the refrigerated section of the supermarket). However, I don't recommend using egg substitute when coating foods for breading. Breading doesn't stick to it very well.

MEATS

• Choose lean cuts of meat and trim away any visible fat before preparing.

- Serve moderate-sized portions, such as 3 to 4 ounces of cooked meat (about 4 to 6 ounces raw) per adult. (That's about the size of a deck of playing cards.)
- Choose cooking methods (like roasting, broiling, grilling, and baking on a rack) that allow fat to drip away during cooking.
- Remove the layer of fat that rises to the top of soups, stews, and pan juices of roasts. Chilling makes this a breeze, so it's even easier to do with dishes that are made ahead and chilled before being reheated. Or, a timesaving tip for removing fat from soups and stews is to simply add a few ice cubes to the warm cooked dish. As soon as the fat sticks to the cubes, remove them, and the fat will come out right along with them!

Ground Beef and Pork

- Select a very lean blend, preferably with a 90 to 10 ratio of lean meat to fat. (Regular ground beef and pork usually have a 70 to 30 ratio.)
- If browning ground beef or pork before adding it to a recipe, after browning, place it in a strainer and rinse it with warm water, then drain and continue as

directed. This should remove most of the excess fat.

- In most recipes, you can replace ground beef or pork with turkey. Keep in mind, though, that ground turkey needs more seasoning than beef or pork.

Sausage

Many markets now offer a variety of lean sausages. This means that there's less fat mixed in with the meat when the sausage is made. Other alternatives to traditional pork or beef sausage are turkey and chicken sausage. Whichever way you go, be sure to read the nutrition label so you know your fat and calorie savings.

CHICKEN

In most recipes, you can substitute boneless and skinless chicken breasts for whole chicken or parts. Remember that boneless breasts are generally thinner, so they'll cook more quickly than bone-in parts; adjust your cooking times accordingly.

DAIRY

Let's look to our supermarket dairy case for some reduced-fat, low-fat, or fat-free alternatives. For instance, there's low-fat milk for our soups and sauces, instead of heavy cream. (Evaporated skim milk will work, too.)

Cream Cheese   Easy—use light or fat-free cream cheese!

Mozzarella Cheese   Many of the low-fat and part-skim mozzarella cheeses taste just as good as the original. They're perfect alternatives, plus you can usually cut down on the amount you use. (We can often reduce the amount of cheese we sprinkle on the tops of casseroles without anybody even noticing!)

Ricotta Cheese   For rich taste while still watching fat in most ricotta recipes, use half regular ricotta and half light or fat-free ricotta. Or, don't hesitate to use all light or fat-free. The choice is yours.

Provolone Cheese   Sure, there are light provolone varieties available. But when I need sliced provolone, I prefer to have the deli slice regular provolone really thin . . . that way I get to use a bit less without sacrificing flavor!

Parmesan Cheese   Parmesan is an excellent choice when watching fat and calories, since its strong flavor means that a little goes a long way! (It's the same with Romano cheese.)

Sour Cream   I often use light versions without missing any flavor but, because sour cream varies widely by brand, I recommend trying several brands until you find the one with the taste and consistency you like best.

SAUCES

Have you seen all the tomato sauces and other tomato products available in the supermarket lately? Not only are there lots of flavors available, but most manufacturers are offering sauces that have less fat and calories, and even ones with less sodium, too. Some of these may be thinner than our "regular" sauces, so you may want to use a bit less of them in casseroles.

A Note About Packaged Foods

Packaged food sizes may vary by brand. Generally, the sizes indicated in these recipes are average sizes. If you can't find the exact package size listed in the ingredients, whatever package is closest in size will usually do the trick.

Cold Salads and Appetizers

Antipasti Freddi

Fresh Mozzarella and Tomato Salad

4 to 6 servings

Fresh, fresh, fresh—that's the word that describes this salad of fresh ripe tomatoes, fresh mozzarella cheese, and fresh basil. It's an Italian classic that you'll find on the Isle of Capri and all across Italy . . . and now on your table, too!

4 medium-sized ripe tomatoes, cut into large chunks
1 pound fresh mozzarella cheese, cut into 1-inch chunks (see page xxii)
½ cup olive oil
¼ cup balsamic vinegar
2 teaspoons chopped fresh basil or ½ teaspoon dried basil
½ teaspoon salt
½ teaspoon black pepper

Place the tomato and mozzarella chunks in a large bowl. Combine the remaining ingredients in a small bowl; mix well. Pour over the tomato and cheese mixture, tossing to coat well. Cover and chill for at least 2 hours before serving.

Tuscan Bread Salad

4 to 5 servings

Tuscany is famous for lots of things, including its classic bread salad. Well, now we can make it at home, too—in just minutes!

10 medium-sized ripe plum
   tomatoes, cut into wedges
3 medium-sized cucumbers,
   peeled and thinly sliced
½ of a red onion, thinly sliced
1 box (5½ ounces) seasoned
   croutons (see Note)

½ cup olive oil
¼ cup balsamic vinegar
½ teaspoon sugar
¼ teaspoon salt
¼ teaspoon black pepper

In a large bowl, combine the tomatoes, cucumbers, onion, and croutons. In a small bowl, whisk together the olive oil, vinegar, sugar, salt, and pepper; pour over the vegetables and croutons. Toss and serve immediately.

NOTE: There are so many different ways to flavor this, simply by changing crouton flavors. Sometimes I use herb-seasoned ones, other times I feel like going with the garlic ones. Try those or whichever ones are your favorites.

Deluxe Antipasto Platter

6 to 8 servings

I call this "deluxe" because it includes a little of this and a little of that—so it can be all our favorites on one platter!

½ pound sliced hard salami
¼ pound sliced capicolla or other spicy ham
6 slices (6 ounces) provolone cheese, cut in half
¼ pound Gorgonzola or other blue cheese, cut into 1-inch cubes
1 can (14 ounces) artichoke hearts, drained and quartered

1 jar (4 ounces) marinated mushrooms, drained
12 peperoncini
¼ pound Sicilian or other green olives, drained
¼ pound Kalamata or other black olives, drained

Arrange the ingredients on a large serving platter as desired, or as follows: Tightly roll the salami slices into tubes and arrange on the platter. Fold the capicolla slices in half, then in half again, and arrange on the platter. Arrange the remaining ingredients on the platter and serve.

NOTE: An antipasto platter can include any of your favorite meats, cheeses, and vegetables, so if capicolla or any of the other items is not available, or if you simply don't want or like them, make substitutions. The platter can be prepared ahead of time, covered, and chilled until ready to serve.

Tortellini Crab Salad

No, you don't have to make the tortellini *or* the dressing from scratch. Don't worry—the tastes in this salad will never give you away!

2 packages (9 ounces each) cheese tortellini
1 package (8 ounces) imitation crabmeat, flaked (see Note)
¼ cup chopped roasted peppers
¾ cup pepper-Parmesan dressing
½ cup sour cream
¼ teaspoon salt
2 tablespoons grated Parmesan cheese

Cook the tortellini according to the package directions; drain, rinse, drain again, then set aside to cool. In a large bowl, combine the remaining ingredients; add the tortellini and mix well. Cover and chill for at least 2 hours before serving.

NOTE: If you prefer, you can drain and flake two 6-ounce cans of lump crabmeat and use that instead of imitation crabmeat.

Little Italy Antipasto

The best Italian chefs would be proud to serve up this hearty version of their traditional meal starter!

1 medium-sized head iceberg lettuce, cut into bite-sized pieces

¼ pound thinly sliced ham, tightly rolled or cut into ½-inch strips

¼ pound thinly sliced Genoa or other hard salami, folded in half or quartered

½ pound fresh mozzarella cheese, cut into 1-inch chunks

2 medium-sized tomatoes, cut into chunks

1 jar (6 ounces) marinated artichoke hearts, drained

1 jar (7 ounces) roasted peppers, drained and cut into ½-inch strips

12 peperoncini

1½ cups extra-large pitted black olives (about 20 olives), drained

½ cup Italian dressing

Cover the bottom of a large platter with the lettuce. Layer the ham, salami, cheese, tomatoes, artichoke hearts, roasted peppers, peperoncini, and olives over the lettuce. Pour the dressing over the salad and serve.

NOTE: Sometimes I like to prepare individual plates of this antipasto and keep them chilled until guests arrive. Then I drizzle each salad with the dressing just before serving.

Artichoke and Shrimp Pasta Salad

6 to 8 servings

My favorite dishes are ones that please the eye as well as the taste buds. This one's a winner in *both* departments!

1 package (12 ounces) tricolored twist pasta
1 bottle (16 ounces) creamy Italian dressing
1 teaspoon dried dillweed
2 cans (14 ounces each) artichoke hearts, drained and quartered

1 package (10 ounces) frozen shrimp, thawed and drained
1 can (2¼ ounces) sliced black olives, drained

Cook the pasta according to the package directions; drain, rinse, drain again, and set aside to cool. In a large bowl, combine the dressing and dillweed. Add the pasta and the remaining ingredients and toss until thoroughly combined. Cover and chill for at least 2 hours before serving.

NOTE: For added crunch, color, and flavor, add a small chopped red onion.

Fast Tuna Antipasto

This is a great light main dish for lunch or supper 'cause it combines a load of garden-fresh ingredients with everybody's favorite . . . tuna!

1 can (12 ounces) tuna, drained
½ of a medium-sized head of iceberg lettuce, coarsely chopped
1 medium-sized tomato, cut into 1-inch chunks
1 medium-sized cucumber, peeled and cut into 1-inch chunks

1 small red onion, cut into 1-inch chunks
1 jar (16 ounces) giardiniera marinated vegetables, drained (see Note)
½ cup Italian dressing

Flake the tuna into a large bowl; add the remaining ingredients and toss until well combined. Serve immediately, or cover and chill until ready to serve.

NOTE: Giardiniera marinated vegetables are a mixture of chunky marinated vegetables such as carrots, cauliflower, and peperoncini and can usually be found near the olives and other marinated vegetables in the supermarket.

Pesto Chicken Salad

6 to 8 servings

We find pesto sauce highlighting so many foods today. That's 'cause it's gone from being considered very fancy to its place now as a mainstream sauce. One taste will tell you why!

½ pound penne pasta
1 container (7 ounces) prepared
    pesto sauce
2 cups chunked cooked chicken

5 plum tomatoes, cut into
    wedges
1 teaspoon salt
1 teaspoon black pepper

Cook the pasta according to the package directions; drain, rinse, drain again, and set aside in a large bowl to cool slightly. Add the pesto sauce and toss to coat. Add the remaining ingredients and toss until thoroughly combined. Cover and chill for at least 2 hours before serving.

NOTE: Any type of leftover chicken can be chunked or cut up to be used in this salad. I especially like to cook up a few extra boneless chicken breasts when I barbecue so I can have them for this recipe.

Marinated Garden Vegetables

My garden happens to be the farm stand that's on my way to work. And whether I pick the veggies myself or not, I love using garden-fresh vegetables for this salad. (Sure, it's okay to mix and match the veggies so that you use only the freshest ones.)

¾ cup vegetable oil
½ cup balsamic vinegar
1 tablespoon Dijon-style mustard
2 teaspoons Worcestershire sauce
2 teaspoons Italian seasoning
½ teaspoon sugar
½ teaspoon salt
2 cups broccoli florets

½ pound fresh mushrooms, quartered
½ pint cherry tomatoes, halved
1 large red onion, cut into ½-inch chunks
1 small zucchini, cut into ½-inch chunks
1 small yellow squash, cut into ½-inch chunks

In a medium-sized saucepan, whisk together the oil, vinegar, mustard, Worcestershire sauce, Italian seasoning, sugar, and salt. Bring to a boil over medium heat and cook for 2 minutes, stirring occasionally. Remove from the heat and let cool to room temperature. Place the remaining ingredients in a large shallow dish and pour the cooled dressing evenly over them. Toss until well coated and combined. Cover and chill for at least 2 hours before serving, tossing occasionally. Toss again just before serving.

Tuna Pasta Salad

6 to 8 servings

In our kitchen, we often toss together a batch of this for lunch. It satisfies all of our king-sized appetites!

1 pound medium-sized pasta shells
1 bottle (8 ounces) Italian dressing
Juice of 1 lemon
1 tablespoon dried oregano
¼ teaspoon salt
¼ teaspoon black pepper

1 can (12 ounces) tuna, drained and flaked
1 can (15½ ounces) garbanzo beans (chick peas), drained
½ cup sun-dried tomatoes in oil, drained and chopped
4 scallions, coarsely chopped

Cook the pasta according to the package directions; drain, rinse, drain again, and set aside to cool. Meanwhile, in a medium-sized bowl, combine the dressing, lemon juice, oregano, salt, and pepper; mix well. In a large bowl, combine the pasta, tuna, garbanzo beans, sun-dried tomatoes, and scallions. Add the dressing mixture and toss until thoroughly combined. Cover and chill for at least 2 hours before serving.

NOTE: I usually use chunk-white tuna packed in water, but whatever tuna is on sale should work! Did you know that sometimes the tuna packed in oil contains less fat than water-packed tuna because it's a less fatty tuna cut? Be sure to check the labels!

Scungilli Salad

4 to 6 servings

"What's scungilli?" you ask. It's a conch-like seafood. And since it's readily available now in cans, this salad is no longer just for special occasions.

1 cup red wine vinegar
½ cup olive oil
3 tablespoons lemon juice
2 teaspoons sugar
2 teaspoons garlic powder
¼ teaspoon crushed red pepper
¼ teaspoon salt
¼ teaspoon black pepper

1 can (28 ounces) scungilli, rinsed, drained, and diced
2 medium-sized bell peppers (1 green and 1 red), diced
1 small red onion, diced
2 scallions, thinly sliced
2 tablespoons chopped fresh parsley

In a large bowl, combine the vinegar, oil, lemon juice, sugar, garlic powder, crushed red pepper, salt, and black pepper; mix well. Add the remaining ingredients and toss until the scungilli is well coated. Cover and marinate in the refrigerator for at least 3 hours before serving, tossing occasionally.

NOTE: I like to make this a day before I plan to serve it so I can be sure the scungilli will be good and marinated—it tastes better that way.

Timely Marinated Mushrooms

4 to 6 servings

I guess you could say that these marinated mushrooms are very timely 'cause they assemble in minutes, marinate for hours, and disappear in seconds!

¾ cup vegetable oil
¼ cup red wine vinegar
6 garlic cloves, minced
1 tablespoon chopped fresh
   parsley

¾ teaspoon salt
½ teaspoon black pepper
1 pound fresh mushrooms,
   quartered
1 large red onion, thinly sliced

In a large bowl, combine the oil, vinegar, garlic, parsley, salt, and pepper; mix until thoroughly combined. Add the remaining ingredients and toss until the mushrooms are evenly coated. Cover and chill for at least 2 hours before serving.

NOTE: If I happen to have any other varieties of mushrooms on hand, such as cremini, porcini, or even portobello, I cut them all to about the same size and include a mix of all of them for truly unbeatable marinated mushrooms.

Prosciutto and Melon Skewers

6 skewers

Prosciutto with melon is no new combination in Italian kitchens. My improvement is to serve it up on skewers so it's lots easier to enjoy that big taste.

1 medium-sized cantaloupe	6 slices (about ¼ pound)
1 teaspoon cracked black	prosciutto
pepper (see Note)	Six 6-inch wooden skewers

Cut the cantaloupe in half and seed it, then cut each half into 4 wedges. Remove the rind and cut each wedge into 3 chunks. In a large bowl, combine the cantaloupe chunks and pepper; mix well. Cut each slice of prosciutto in half lengthwise, then in half crosswise. Wrap a piece of prosciutto around each chunk of cantaloupe, overlapping the ends. Place 4 chunks on each skewer, making sure that the ends of the prosciutto are pierced and not hanging loose, and serve; or cover and chill until ready to serve.

NOTE: You can buy cracked black pepper in the spice section of your supermarket or you can place whole peppercorns in a resealable plastic storage bag and crack them with a mallet. You could use ground black pepper instead, but ⅛ to ¼ teaspoon would be enough.

Anchovy Potato Salad

4 to 6 servings

I know you're thinking, "Anchovies in potato salad?!" Yup—they add a little wow to each forkful.

6 medium-sized red-skinned potatoes (about 2 pounds), cut into ⅛-inch slices
1 teaspoon salt
1 medium-sized green bell pepper, coarsely chopped
1 medium-sized onion, thinly sliced

1 bottle (8 ounces) Italian salad dressing
1 can (2 ounces) anchovy fillets, rinsed, drained, and coarsely chopped
¼ teaspoon black pepper

Place the potatoes and salt in a large pot and fill with just enough water to cover the potatoes. Bring to a boil over high heat and cook for 5 minutes, or until the potatoes are fork-tender. Drain the potatoes and immediately place them in a large bowl of ice water to cool; drain again. Place the potatoes in the large bowl and add the remaining ingredients; toss until the potatoes are well coated. Cover and chill for at least 2 hours before serving.

NOTE: For a more colorful salad, sometimes I use half of a yellow bell pepper and half of a green bell pepper instead of just a whole green one.

Caponata

4 to 6 servings

Here's a Sicilian favorite that's welcome as a meal starter *and* as a party snack. Just serve it up with crackers or sliced Italian bread.

2 tablespoons olive or
   vegetable oil
1 large eggplant (about 1½
   pounds), coarsely chopped
1 medium-sized onion,
   chopped
2 tablespoons garlic powder
½ teaspoon salt
½ cup green olives, pitted and
   coarsely chopped

3 celery stalks, chopped
1 can (8 ounces) tomato sauce
¼ cup white vinegar
⅓ cup firmly packed light
   brown sugar
2 or 3 dashes hot pepper sauce
   (optional)

In a large saucepan, heat the oil over medium-high heat and add the eggplant, onion, garlic powder, and salt; sauté for about 5 minutes, until the eggplant begins to soften, stirring occasionally. Stir in the remaining ingredients and cook over medium-high heat for 25 to 30 minutes, until the vegetables begin to get mushy. Allow to cool, then cover and chill until ready to use.

NOTE: If your eggplant is bitter, you may want to add an additional 1 to 2 tablespoons of brown sugar while it's cooking.

Classic Bruschetta

8 to 10 slices

Bruschetta is simply a fancy way to say "toasted bread with a tasty topping." See? With each new recipe we learn more and more Italian!

1 loaf (1 pound) Italian bread, cut in half lengthwise
⅓ cup olive oil
⅓ cup chopped fresh basil or 2 tablespoons dried basil
1 teaspoon salt
1 teaspoon black pepper
10 medium-sized plum tomatoes, seeded and chopped

Preheat the broiler. Place the bread cut side up on a baking sheet and broil for 2 to 3 minutes, or until golden. Place on a large serving platter. In a large bowl, combine the remaining ingredients; mix until well blended, then spoon over the toasted bread. Cut and serve.

NOTE: If you prefer, the bread can be sliced first and then toasted to create individual bruschetta. To seed the plum tomatoes, cut them in half lengthwise and gently squeeze to release the seeds.

Hot Appetizers
Antipasti Calde

continued

Stuffed Baby Eggplant

4 to 6 servings

These stuffed eggplants are so good because you use *baby* eggplant, which cooks up nice and tender.

6 baby eggplant, stems removed (see Note)
2 tablespoons olive oil
1 medium-sized onion, finely chopped
½ of a green bell pepper, finely chopped
1 can (14½ ounces) diced tomatoes, drained

1 teaspoon garlic powder
½ cup seasoned bread crumbs
1 cup (4 ounces) shredded mozzarella cheese, divided
½ teaspoon salt
1 can (5.5 ounces) vegetable or tomato juice

Preheat the oven to 350°F. Cut the eggplant in half lengthwise; scoop out the pulp and coarsely chop it. In a large skillet, heat the olive oil over medium-low heat and add the chopped eggplant, onion, pepper, tomatoes, and garlic powder. Cook for 15 to 20 minutes, or until the vegetables are tender, stirring occasionally. Stir in the bread crumbs, ½ cup mozzarella cheese, the salt, and vegetable juice; cook for 2 to 3 minutes, until the liquid is absorbed. Remove from the heat and cool slightly. Spoon the vegetable mixture evenly into the eggplant shells. Place in a 9″ × 13″ baking dish that has been coated with nonstick cooking spray. Cover with aluminum foil and bake for 1 hour. Remove the foil, sprinkle with the remaining ½ cup mozzarella cheese, and bake for 20 to 25 minutes, or until the eggplant is tender.

NOTE: Use baby eggplant that are about 6 inches long. Eggplant that are much smaller or larger won't come out the same!

Crispy Zucchini Strips

48 strips

We've all had fried eggplant, and now it's time to give zucchini a turn. You'll be glad you did!

3 medium-sized zucchini
  (about 1 pound total)
1 teaspoon salt
½ cup all-purpose flour
1½ cups Italian-flavored bread
  crumbs

2 eggs
2 tablespoons milk
2 cups vegetable oil

Cut each zucchini in half crosswise, then cut each half into 8 long strips. Place the zucchini in a medium-sized bowl and sprinkle with the salt; toss to coat evenly. Place the flour and bread crumbs in separate shallow dishes. In another shallow dish, whisk together the eggs and milk. Coat each zucchini strip in the flour, dip in the egg mixture, and then coat completely with the bread crumbs; set aside on a platter. In a large skillet, heat the oil over medium-high heat until hot but not smoking. Fry the zucchini strips a few at a time for 3 to 4 minutes, until golden on all sides, turning frequently. Drain on paper towels and serve immediately.

NOTE: If you cook these in a table-top deep fryer, they come out really crisp and golden.

Sausage-Stuffed Mushrooms

12 mushrooms

These are so easy to make that you'll want to have a party just to try them out! I love 'em for those spur-of-the-moment drop-ins . . . or anytime I want a no-fuss appetizer that'll rise above the rest.

1 pound medium-sized fresh mushrooms (see Note)
¼ pound bulk hot Italian sausage
¼ cup Italian-flavored bread crumbs
¼ cup sour cream
⅛ teaspoon garlic powder

Select the 12 largest mushrooms; remove the stems and reserve the caps. Finely chop the stems, along with the remaining mushrooms. In a large skillet, combine the chopped mushrooms and sausage over medium-high heat and cook for 4 to 5 minutes, or until no pink remains in the sausage, stirring frequently to break up the sausage. Remove from the heat and stir in the bread crumbs, sour cream, and garlic powder until well combined. Preheat the broiler. Spoon the mixture evenly into the reserved mushroom caps and place on a rimmed baking sheet. Broil for 4 to 6 minutes, or until lightly browned.

NOTE: When making stuffed mushrooms, you want to make sure to use mushrooms that are all about the same size.

Quick Roasted Peppers

3 to 4 servings

These are a must-have 'cause bell peppers are always available, usually inexpensive, and come in a range of beautiful colors. Oh, yeah—we can eat this classic standby hot or cold.

2 tablespoons vegetable oil
¼ teaspoon onion powder
¼ teaspoon garlic powder
¼ teaspoon salt
¼ teaspoon black pepper
4 large bell peppers (2 green and 2 red), quartered

Preheat the oven to 450°F. In a medium-sized bowl, combine all the ingredients except the peppers; mix well. Add the peppers to the bowl and toss to coat well. Place the peppers on a baking sheet and roast for 20 to 25 minutes, or until tender.

NOTE: These are perfect for those times when you have extra bell peppers or when you get them on sale. And for extra color and flavor, add some yellow or orange bell peppers.

Artichoke Croquettes

Mamma mia! All we need is a little marinara sauce for dipping and we're on our way. . . .

1 tablespoon butter
1 medium-sized onion, finely
  chopped
¾ cup plus 1 tablespoon all-
  purpose flour, divided
1 can (14 ounces) artichoke
  hearts, well drained and
  finely chopped
1 teaspoon chopped fresh
  parsley

2 egg yolks
¼ teaspoon salt
1 egg
1 tablespoon milk
¾ cup Italian-flavored bread
  crumbs
2 cups vegetable oil

In a large skillet, melt the butter over medium heat and sauté the onion for 2 to 3 minutes, or until tender. Stir in 1 tablespoon flour until blended. Remove from the heat and allow to cool slightly, then stir in the artichokes, parsley, egg yolks, and salt. Place the remaining ¾ cup flour in a shallow dish. In another shallow dish, whisk together the egg and milk. Place the bread crumbs in a third shallow dish. Dip the artichoke mixture by tablespoonfuls into the flour, then into the egg mixture, and then into the bread crumbs, coating completely. Shape into 3-inch croquette logs and set aside on a platter. In a large skillet, heat the oil over high heat until hot but not smoking. Cook the croquettes in batches (to avoid crowding), for 3 to 4 minutes, or until golden brown, turning to brown on all sides. Drain on paper towels and serve immediately.

Stuffed Artichoke Flowers

4 servings

If you've never eaten stuffed artichokes, you're in for a real treat! The savory stuffing tucked between the tender leaves is as tasty as it is fun to eat.

4 large artichokes, trimmed
¼ teaspoon salt
¼ cup olive oil, divided
4 tablespoons (½ stick) butter
1 medium-sized onion, chopped

2 teaspoons minced garlic
1 cup Italian-flavored bread crumbs
1 teaspoon grated Parmesan cheese

Place the artichokes and salt in a large pot and fill the pot with just enough water to cover the artichokes. Bring to a boil over

high heat and cook for 35 to 40 minutes, or until the artichokes are tender. Remove the artichokes and allow to drain upside down; place in an 8-inch square baking dish and set aside. Preheat the oven to 375°F. In a medium-sized skillet, heat 3 tablespoons oil and the butter over medium heat; add the onion and sprinkle with the garlic. Cook for 3 minutes, or until the onion is tender. Remove from the heat and stir in the bread crumbs and Parmesan cheese. Spread the artichoke leaves apart and fill the spaces between the leaves with the stuffing mixture. Sprinkle the remaining 1 tablespoon olive oil over the artichokes. Cover tightly with aluminum foil and bake for 15 to 20 minutes, or until hot. Serve immediately.

NOTE: Pull off each artichoke leaf and eat only the pulp by removing it with your teeth. Oh—and for added flavor, squeeze half of a lemon into the boiling water with the artichokes.

Confetti Portobello Mushrooms

6 servings

The popularity of this veggie is really mushrooming! And once you taste this meaty appetizer studded with sautéed peppers and onions, you'll know why!

3 tablespoons olive oil
2 large bell peppers (1 green and 1 red), cut into ½-inch strips
1 large onion, cut into wedges

½ teaspoon garlic powder
1 teaspoon salt
½ teaspoon black pepper
6 large portobello mushroom caps

In a large skillet, heat the oil over medium-high heat; add the bell peppers and onion, sprinkle with the garlic powder, salt, and black pepper, and sauté for 5 to 7 minutes, or until the peppers are tender, mixing well. Add the mushrooms and cook for 7 to 10 minutes, or until the mushrooms are heated through and tender, turning halfway through the cooking.

NOTE: Why not turn this appetizer into a really unusual sandwich? Serve each mushroom cap on a crusty roll, topped with the sautéed peppers and onions.

Baked Eggplant Parmigiana Chips

about 24 chips

Since eggplant is related to the potato, it's a natural step to make chips out of eggplant, too! But these are no ordinary chips . . . they're hot and bubbly and come complete with baked-on dip.

3 eggs
½ teaspoon salt
¼ teaspoon black pepper
2 cups Italian-flavored bread crumbs
1 large eggplant, peeled and cut into ¼-inch rounds

Nonstick cooking spray
2 cups spaghetti sauce
1 cup (4 ounces) shredded mozzarella cheese

Preheat the oven to 350°F. In a shallow dish, beat the eggs with the salt and pepper. Place the bread crumbs in another shallow dish. Line 2 large baking sheets with aluminum foil and coat generously with nonstick cooking spray; set aside. Dip each slice of eggplant in the egg mixture, then in the bread crumbs, coating completely. Place the slices on the baking sheets in a single layer, then spray the tops with nonstick cooking spray. Bake for 15 minutes, then turn the slices over and bake for 15 more minutes. Remove from the oven and place 1 tablespoon spaghetti sauce on each. Sprinkle evenly with the mozzarella cheese and return to the oven for 4 to 5 more minutes, or until the sauce is bubbly and the cheese has melted.

NOTE: You can substitute other kinds of cheese, if you'd prefer—and if you don't want to use spaghetti sauce, just leave it out!

Vegetable Turnovers

Using store-bought pastry means you can turn out these turnovers in a snap. And just watch—they'll be snapped up before you can turn around!

2 tablespoons olive oil
1 large sweet onion, thinly sliced
1 large green bell pepper, cut into thin strips
3 garlic cloves, minced
10 sun-dried tomatoes, reconstituted according to the package directions and sliced

1 can (2¼ ounces) sliced black olives, drained
3 tablespoons tomato paste
½ teaspoon salt
1 package (17¼ ounces) frozen puff pastry (2 sheets), thawed
1 egg
1 tablespoon water

Preheat the oven to 375°F. In a large skillet, heat the olive oil over medium-low heat. Add the onion and bell pepper and cook for about 15 minutes, or until the vegetables are tender. Add the garlic, sun-dried tomatoes, olives, tomato paste, and salt. Cook for 15 more minutes; remove from the heat and allow to cool completely. On a lightly floured surface, roll out each pastry sheet with a rolling pin to a 12-inch square. Cut each diagonally into quarters, making 8 triangles in all. Spoon the vegetable mixture evenly into the center of the dough triangles and fold the dough over the filling, forming 8 turnovers. Pinch the edges to seal, moistening them with water if necessary. In a shallow dish, beat the egg and water until well blended. Brush the tops of the turnovers with the egg mixture and place on rimmed baking sheets that have been coated with nonstick cooking spray. Bake for 20 to 25 minutes, or until golden brown; serve.

Sesame Artichokes

about 30 pieces

Just as the heart of all Italian towns is the central square, these tender artichoke hearts will surely be the center of attraction on your dinner table.

½ cup Italian-flavored bread crumbs
⅓ cup sesame seeds
3 tablespoons grated Parmesan cheese
½ teaspoon salt

¼ teaspoon black pepper
2 eggs, lightly beaten
2 cans (14 ounces each) artichoke hearts, drained and cut in half
1½ cups vegetable oil

In a shallow dish, combine the bread crumbs, sesame seeds, Parmesan cheese, salt, and pepper; mix well. Place the eggs in another shallow dish. Dip each artichoke piece in the eggs, then roll in the bread crumb mixture, coating evenly; set aside on a plate. In a large skillet, heat the oil over medium-high heat until hot but not smoking. Cook the artichokes in small batches for about 1 minute, or until golden brown, turning to brown all sides. Remove with a slotted spoon and drain on paper towels. Serve immediately.

NOTE: These are great plain or served with spicy brown mustard for dipping.

Crispy Mozzarella Sticks

12 sticks

Chewy, stretchy, and crunchy . . . Who could ask for better than that in a finger food?!

¼ cup all-purpose flour
1 cup Italian-flavored bread
  crumbs
2 eggs
1 tablespoon milk

1 package (9 ounces)
  mozzarella string cheese
  (12 pieces)
2 cups vegetable oil

Place the flour and bread crumbs in separate shallow dishes. In another shallow dish, whisk together the eggs and milk. Coat each piece of string cheese in the flour, then dip in the egg mixture and coat completely with the bread crumbs. Dip the coated cheese in the egg mixture again and coat with a second layer of bread crumbs; place on a platter. In a large skillet, heat the oil over medium-high heat until hot but not smoking. Carefully place the coated cheese in the hot oil and cook for about 1 minute, or until golden brown, turning to brown all sides. Drain on paper towels and serve immediately.

NOTE: Serve with warmed marinara sauce or one of your favorite dipping sauces.

Fontina Fondue

This is a take-off on *fonduta,* the classic Italian dish made with fontina cheese, milk, egg yolks, and truffles (similar to mushrooms). Nobody said we have to be traditional, did they?

½ pound fontina cheese, cut into ½-inch cubes
½ cup half-and-half
2 tablespoons butter
½ teaspoon salt
2 egg yolks
1 loaf (1 pound) Italian bread, cut into 1-inch cubes

In a medium-sized saucepan, combine the cheese, half-and-half, butter, and salt. Cook over low heat for 6 to 7 minutes, or until the cheese is melted, stirring occasionally. Beat the egg yolks in a small bowl. Add 2 to 3 tablespoons of the hot cheese mixture to the beaten egg yolks and mix well. Whisk the egg yolk mixture into the cheese mixture and cook for 3 to 4 minutes, or until the mixture has thickened, stirring constantly. Place in a fondue pot over heat or in a heat-proof serving bowl on a warming tray. Serve with the bread cubes for dunking.

NOTE: Go crazy with your dippers . . . use chunks of apple, cooked chicken, or even crispy bread sticks.

Fresh Pizza Biscuits

20 biscuits

Get everything you always wanted on a pizza, including that fresh-from-the-oven taste—without waiting for the delivery van!

1 package (10.8 ounces) refrigerated flaky buttermilk biscuits (5 biscuits) (see Note)
1 cup (4 ounces) shredded mozzarella cheese
3 medium-sized plum tomatoes, each cut into about 7 slices
2 teaspoons chopped fresh basil

Preheat the oven to 350°F. With your fingers, separate each biscuit into 4 layers and place on two 10″ × 15″ baking sheets. Bake for 7 to 8 minutes, or until the biscuits are golden. Remove the biscuits from the oven and top each with some cheese, a tomato slice, and a sprinkle of basil. Return to the oven and bake for 7 to 8 minutes, or until the cheese is melted.

NOTE: Make sure to buy the flaky-style biscuits so you can separate the layers into thin biscuits; regular biscuits can't easily be separated into layers. For added flavor, combine ¼ teaspoon garlic powder and 2 tablespoons grated Parmesan cheese and sprinkle over the tops before baking.

Spinach Bruschetta

20 to 24 slices

This special bread used to be a well-kept secret, known only to Italian families. But we broke the code and made it a front-runner at all of *our* Italian dinners.

1 loaf (1 pound) Italian bread, cut into ½-inch slices
1 tablespoon olive oil
3 garlic cloves, minced
1 package (10 ounces) frozen chopped spinach, thawed and well drained

¼ teaspoon crushed red pepper
1 cup (4 ounces) shredded mozzarella cheese, divided
½ cup grated Parmesan cheese

Preheat the oven to 375°F. Place the bread slices on 2 large rimmed baking sheets and set aside. In a large skillet, heat the olive oil over medium-high heat. Add the garlic, spinach, and crushed red pepper. Reduce the heat to medium and cook for 3 to 4 minutes, or until the garlic is golden. Add ¾ cup mozzarella cheese and the Parmesan cheese, stirring to blend. Cook for 1 to 2 more minutes, or until the cheese melts; remove from the heat. Spread the spinach mixture evenly over the bread and top with the remaining ¼ cup mozzarella cheese. Bake for 4 to 5 minutes, or until the bread is golden and the cheese has melted.

NOTE: You can also start with a 10-ounce package of fresh spinach that has been washed and trimmed, but it will take longer to sauté and you may need to add a little more oil. Once it's cooked, proceed as above.

"My Way" Bruschetta

24 to 30 slices

No "knead" to go to a lot of trouble if you do this my way! Taste the comfort of homemade Italian bread topped with yummy cheese and seasonings. They'll applaud and say, "Mmm mmm . . . *Molto bene!*" (Very good!)

1 loaf (1 pound) Italian bread, cut in half lengthwise
⅓ cup olive oil
1 garlic clove, minced
¼ teaspoon salt
¼ teaspoon black pepper
4 scallions, thinly sliced
1 small tomato, chopped
1½ cups (6 ounces) shredded mozzarella cheese

Preheat the oven to 500°F. Place the bread cut side up on a foil-lined baking sheet; set aside. In a small bowl, combine the olive oil, garlic, salt, and pepper. Drizzle the mixture over the cut sides of the bread. Sprinkle the bread with the scallions and tomato, then top with the cheese. Bake for 5 to 7 minutes, or until the cheese melts and begins to turn golden brown. Cut into 1-inch slices and serve.

NOTE: For an even cheesier bruschetta, sprinkle with ¼ cup grated Parmesan cheese before topping with the mozzarella cheese.

Old World Chicken Livers

4 servings

How many times have you cleared a room when you announced you were serving liver? Well, those days are over, 'cause with one taste of these tender, flavorful morsels, fans will be flocking to your feet!

3 tablespoons butter
1 pound chicken livers
1 small onion, finely chopped
½ cup dry white wine
½ teaspoon dried sage

½ teaspoon salt
⅛ teaspoon black pepper
2 tablespoons chopped fresh
   parsley

In a large skillet, melt the butter over medium heat. Add the livers and onion and sauté for 3 to 4 minutes, or until no pink remains in the livers. Add the wine, sage, salt, and pepper and increase the heat to high. Cook for 10 to 12 minutes, or until the liquid has evaporated, stirring occasionally. Sprinkle with the parsley and serve.

NOTE: Serve with crackers or on toasted bread.

Cheesy Chicken Croquettes

about 18 croquettes

A little of the unexpected in the form of Italian cheeses turns these ordinary chicken croquettes into our ticket to a Roman holiday!

1½ cups water
¾ cup long- or whole-grain
   white rice
1 small onion, finely chopped
1 teaspoon salt, divided
2 cans (10 ounces each)
   chicken, drained and flaked
½ cup (2 ounces) shredded
   mozzarella cheese

¼ cup grated Romano cheese
2 eggs
¼ cup chopped fresh parsley
½ teaspoon black pepper
1 cup Italian-flavored bread
   crumbs
2 cups vegetable oil

In a medium-sized saucepan, combine the water, rice, onion, and ½ teaspoon salt. Bring to a boil over high heat, then cover and reduce the heat to low. Simmer for 15 minutes, or until almost tender. Remove from the heat and let cool for 10 minutes, covered. Stir in the chicken, the mozzarella and Romano cheeses, the eggs, parsley, pepper, and the remaining ½ teaspoon salt; mix well. Place the bread crumbs in a shallow dish. Form the rice mixture into patties, using ¼ cup of the mixture for each; coat with the bread crumbs and place on a platter. In a large deep skillet, heat the oil over high heat until hot but not smoking. Carefully place a few of the patties in the hot oil and cook for 5 to 6 minutes, or until golden, turning halfway through the cooking. Drain on paper towels and cook the remaining croquettes in batches.

NOTE: These can be served Parmigiana-style by topping the fried croquettes with some spaghetti sauce and a sprinkling of mozzarella cheese, then baking in a 350°F. oven until the croquettes are warmed through and the cheese is melted.

Mussels Marinara

The first time I heard the song "Molly Malone," I wondered what cockles and mussels were. Well, I haven't tried cockles, but boy, have I fallen in love with mussels . . . especially ones fixed this way!

2 pounds fresh mussels, cleaned (see Note)	¼ cup dry white wine
1 can (14½ ounces) stewed tomatoes, chopped, juice reserved	½ teaspoon dried oregano
	1 teaspoon salt
	¼ teaspoon black pepper

Combine all the ingredients (including the juice from the tomatoes) in a large pot. Cover and bring to a boil over high heat; reduce the heat to low and simmer for 6 to 8 minutes, or until the mussels open. Do not overcook. **Discard any mussels that do not open.** Remove to a serving platter or individual serving bowls and serve.

NOTE: Some fish markets sell mussels already cleaned and ready for cooking. If you buy mussels that aren't prepared, here's what to do: Wash them under cold running water and scrub away any grit or barnacles with a stiff food scrub brush. Remove the black "beard" from each mussel by cutting or pulling it off.

Fried Calamari

2 to 4 servings

The first time I tried squid in a restaurant, I was about twenty years old, and I did it on a dare from a friend. I closed my eyes, opened my mouth, and took a bite. What a surprise! I really liked it! I learned my first lesson about trying out new foods . . . and that was the beginning of my passion for trying all sorts of exotic foods!

1 pound cleaned calamari
   (squid) (see Note)
¾ cup all-purpose flour

½ teaspoon salt
½ teaspoon black pepper
1 cup vegetable oil

Cut the tube-like calamari bodies into ½-inch rings, leaving the tentacles intact. In a large resealable plastic storage bag, combine the flour, salt, and pepper. Add the calamari in small batches and toss until completely coated with the flour mixture. Heat the oil in a large deep skillet over medium-high heat until hot but not smoking. Fry the calamari in small batches for 4 to 6 minutes, or until golden brown. Drain on paper towels and serve immediately.

NOTE: Serve with a warm marinara sauce for dipping. Oh—I always make sure to buy the calamari already cleaned so that all I have to do is cut it up when I get home.

Clams Casino Royale

24 clams

No matter how you roll the dice, these'll turn out to be winning starters for any bash!

¼ pound bacon
½ of a small red bell pepper, coarsely chopped
2 garlic cloves
¼ cup Italian-flavored bread crumbs

1 tablespoon grated Parmesan cheese
2 dozen littleneck clams (see Note)

In a food processor that has been fitted with its metal cutting blade, combine the bacon, red pepper, and garlic; process until smooth. Add the bread crumbs and cheese and continue to process until thoroughly mixed and the mixture holds together; set aside. Meanwhile, in a large pot, bring 2 inches of water to a boil. Place the clams in the boiling water and cover. Steam the clams for 5 to 8 minutes, or until they open. Remove from the pot and place on a platter. **Discard any clams that do not open.** Preheat the broiler. Remove the top shells of the clams and discard, leaving the clams in the bottom halves of the shells. Divide the bread crumb mixture evenly among the clams, spreading it to completely cover them. Place on a baking sheet and broil for 4 to 6 minutes, or until the topping is cooked through.

NOTE: Larger clams can be used, but you may have to double the quantity of filling ingredients.

Soups
Zuppe

Pasta e Fagiole	45
Italian Chicken Soup	46
Tortellini Soup	47
White Bean Soup	48
Chick Pea and Pasta Soup	49
Hearty Minestrone	50
Quick Spinach-Parmesan Soup	51
Simple Escarole Soup	52
Broccoli Rabe Soup	53
Lentil Soup	54
Thick-and-Hearty Pepper Soup	55
Spinach-Potato Soup	56
Spicy Sausage and Bean Soup	57
Creamy Tomato Soup	58
Artichoke and Fennel Soup	59
Zucchini Cream Soup	60

Pasta e Fagiole

Boy, do I ever have memories of my neighbor serving up piping-hot bowls full of thick flavorful broth and loads of macaroni and beans. And these days, when I get a longing for that satisfying good taste, I just simmer up some of my own *pasta e fagiole* (American pronunciation: pasta fah-zool!) and it's ready in a jiffy!

2 tablespoons olive oil
2 medium-sized onions, chopped
6 garlic cloves, minced
3 cans (14½ ounces each) ready-to-use chicken broth
2 cans (20 ounces each) cannellini beans, undrained
1 can (14½ ounces) diced tomatoes, undrained
½ teaspoon salt
1 teaspoon black pepper
1 cup uncooked ditalini pasta (see Note)
½ cup chopped fresh parsley

In a large soup pot, heat the oil over medium heat and sauté the onions and garlic for about 10 minutes, or until the onions are tender. Stir in the chicken broth, 1 can of cannellini beans, the tomatoes, salt, and pepper; cook for 30 minutes, stirring occasionally. Meanwhile, cook the pasta according to the package directions and drain. Using a potato masher, gently mash the beans and tomatoes in the soup pot. Add the remaining can of beans, the parsley, and the cooked pasta. Reduce the heat to low and simmer for 30 minutes, stirring occasionally.

NOTE: Ditalini is a small tube-shaped pasta that's perfect here, but any other type of small pasta can be used.

Italian Chicken Soup

8 to 10 servings

Forget the big pot simmering on the stove for hours, and don't worry about boning the chicken either. Instead, enjoy the quick ease of this toss-together.

7 cups water
6 cans (10½ ounces each)
   condensed chicken broth
2 medium-sized onions, finely
   chopped
4 medium-sized carrots, finely
   chopped

1 bay leaf
⅛ teaspoon ground cinnamon
⅛ teaspoon ground cloves
⅛ teaspoon crushed red pepper
8 ounces orzo or acini di pepe
   pasta
1 cup grated Romano cheese

In a large soup pot, combine the water, chicken broth, onions, carrots, bay leaf, cinnamon, cloves, and red pepper and bring to a boil over high heat. Reduce the heat to low, cover, and simmer for 30 minutes, stirring occasionally. **Remove and discard the bay leaf.** Return to a boil, then add the pasta and cook for 8 to 10 minutes, or until the pasta is tender. Just before serving, stir in the Romano cheese.

NOTE: If you're not planning to serve all the soup right away, then add the cheese to each individual serving bowl instead of stirring it into the whole batch.

Tortellini Soup

Thank heaven for the freezer case! This would take hours if we made the tortellini from scratch, instead of the minutes it takes when we get frozen tortellini from the supermarket.

2 tablespoons olive oil
1 medium-sized onion,
　chopped
2 cans (14½ ounces each)
　diced tomatoes, undrained
2 tablespoons balsamic vinegar
2 garlic cloves, chopped
¼ teaspoon dried oregano
¼ teaspoon salt

¼ teaspoon black pepper
4 cups water
3 cans (10½ ounces each)
　condensed chicken broth
1 package (14 ounces) frozen
　or refrigerated cheese
　tortellini
2 tablespoons chopped fresh
　basil

In a large soup pot, heat the oil over medium-high heat. Sauté the onion until tender, then add the tomatoes, vinegar, garlic, oregano, salt, and pepper; cook for 5 to 7 minutes, or until heated through. Add the water and broth and bring to a boil. Add the tortellini and basil and cook for 6 to 8 minutes, or until the tortellini is tender. Serve immediately.

NOTE: Remember, there are lots of different types of fresh tortellini that are filled with all sorts of yummies like smoked sausage and four-cheese blends. Go ahead and try different ones here.

White Bean Soup

This recipe comes from Beantown—actually, from Boston's North End, where you can have some of the world's truly best meals . . . from soup to sweets!

¼ cup olive oil
1 medium-sized onion, finely chopped
1½ cups water
1 can (20 ounces) cannellini beans, undrained
1 can (16 ounces) navy beans, undrained

1 can (15½ ounces) Great Northern beans, undrained
2 chicken bouillon cubes
1 teaspoon Italian seasoning
½ teaspoon garlic powder

In a large soup pot, heat the oil over medium-high heat. Sauté the onion for 5 to 6 minutes, or until golden. Add the remaining ingredients and bring to a boil. Reduce the heat to medium-low and simmer for 8 to 10 minutes, or until heated through.

NOTE: The sizes of cans of beans vary by manufacturer; as long as the sizes are about the same, this recipe will come out fine.

Chick Pea and Pasta Soup

There are endless regional versions of chicken soup—you know, the favorite comfort food—and they can all give us that warm cozy feeling of home. We can try a different version each time we make it, just by adding one or two special touches, like the chick peas in this one.

1 tablespoon vegetable oil
2 medium-sized onions,
 chopped
1 garlic clove, minced
3 cans (14½ ounces each)
 ready-to-use chicken broth
1 can (15 ounces) chick peas
 (garbanzo beans), undrained

2 cups chopped cooked chicken
1 cup uncooked ditalini or
 other medium-sized pasta
 shape
2 tablespoons chopped fresh
 parsley
½ teaspoon salt
½ teaspoon black pepper

In a large soup pot, heat the oil over medium heat. Sauté the onions and garlic for 3 to 5 minutes, or until tender. Add the remaining ingredients and cook for 12 to 15 minutes, or until the pasta is tender. Serve immediately.

Hearty Minestrone

The most Italian of all soups—the word *minestrone* actually translates as soup!

3 cans (14½ ounces each) ready-to-use beef broth
1 can (15 ounces) red kidney beans, undrained
1 can (20 ounces) cannellini beans, undrained
1 can (28 ounces) crushed tomatoes
1 package (10 ounces) frozen chopped spinach, thawed

1 package (10 ounces) frozen mixed vegetables, thawed
1 small onion, chopped
1 teaspoon garlic powder
1 teaspoon salt
½ teaspoon black pepper
1 cup uncooked elbow macaroni

In a large soup pot, combine all the ingredients except the macaroni. Bring to a boil over medium-high heat, then stir in the macaroni. Reduce the heat to low and simmer for 30 minutes, or until the macaroni is tender, stirring occasionally.

NOTE: Why not top each bowl with a little grated Parmesan cheese? It'll give your minestrone a richer taste, spoonful after spoonful.

Quick Spinach-Parmesan Soup

8 to 10 servings

In Italian, this is called *stracciatella alla romana*. In my house we simply call it one of our favorites!

6 cans (10½ ounces each) condensed chicken broth
6 cups water
5 ounces fresh spinach, washed, trimmed, and chopped

¾ cup grated Parmesan cheese
2 eggs, beaten

In a large soup pot, bring the chicken broth and water to a boil over high heat. Add the spinach and cook for 4 to 5 minutes, or until the spinach is tender. Stir in the cheese, then gradually stir in the beaten eggs so they form strands. Serve immediately.

NOTE: You can turn this into a dish popular with some Italians by dropping a couple dozen marble-sized meatballs into the soup and cooking them in the boiling broth. Oh—for a nice finishing touch, sprinkle each bowl with some freshly grated Parmesan cheese.

Simple Escarole Soup

4 to 6 servings

To many of us, escarole is one of those mysterious vegetables (actually, it's considered an herb) that we're not sure how to use. Don't be intimidated! Start off with this easy soup, and you'll never be without escarole again!

3 cans (14½ ounces each)
   ready-to-use chicken broth
½ pound ground beef
2 tablespoons grated Parmesan
   cheese
¼ teaspoon garlic powder

¼ teaspoon salt
⅛ teaspoon black pepper
1 small head escarole or ½ of a
   medium-sized head, washed,
   drained, and coarsely
   chopped

In a large soup pot, heat the chicken broth over medium-high heat. Meanwhile, in a small bowl, combine the ground beef, Parmesan cheese, garlic powder, salt, and pepper. Roll the beef mixture into teaspoon-sized meatballs. Place the meatballs in the broth and bring to a boil. Reduce the heat to low and simmer for 10 to 12 minutes, or until the meatballs are cooked through. Add the escarole and cook for 8 to 10 minutes, or until tender. Serve immediately.

NOTE: You can add 1 to 2 cups cooked rice with the escarole if you'd like a more filling soup.

Broccoli Rabe Soup

5 to 6 servings

Broccoli rabe, rapini . . . there are lots of names and pronunciations for this leafy broccoli. It has a slightly bitter flavor that makes it a nice change from traditional broccoli. Try it and see if you agree!

¼ cup olive oil
1 medium-sized onion, chopped
2 medium-sized carrots, chopped
1 pound broccoli rabe, trimmed and cut into 1-inch pieces

6 cups water
4 beef bouillon cubes
½ teaspoon salt
½ teaspoon black pepper
½ cup uncooked mini shell pasta

In a large soup pot, heat the olive oil over medium-high heat and sauté the onion, carrots, and broccoli rabe for 5 to 6 minutes, or until tender. Add the remaining ingredients except the pasta and bring to a boil. Stir in the pasta, then reduce the heat to medium and cook for 8 to 10 minutes, or until the pasta is tender, stirring occasionally.

Lentil Soup

My health-conscious friends are always telling me how good lentils are for us. This soup has such great taste that that's a welcome bonus!

2 tablespoons olive oil
1 medium-sized onion, chopped
3 garlic cloves, minced
5 cups water
2 cans (14½ ounces each) ready-to-use chicken broth
1 package (12 ounces) dried lentils, washed and drained

3 medium-sized carrots, finely chopped
2 bay leaves
¼ teaspoon dried rosemary
1 teaspoon salt
¾ teaspoon black pepper

In a large soup pot, heat the oil over medium heat and sauté the onion and garlic for 3 minutes. Add the remaining ingredients and bring to a boil over medium-high heat. Reduce the heat to low, cover, and simmer for 40 to 45 minutes, or until the lentils are tender. **Remove and discard the bay leaves before serving.**

NOTE: For a heartier soup, add about 1 cup of chopped smoked ham or leftover cooked beef, or even chopped cold cuts, along with the other ingredients.

Thick-and-Hearty Pepper Soup

5 to 6 servings

There's more than one way to make sure that gang of yours eats their veggies . . . disguise 'em! Just one taste of this creamy rich soup will have them wanting more, more, more!

4 large yellow bell peppers, chopped
1 medium-sized onion, chopped
3 tablespoons olive oil
1 teaspoon salt
¼ teaspoon black pepper
2 cans (14½ ounces each) ready-to-use chicken broth
1 large potato, peeled and cut into ½-inch cubes
2 celery stalks, chopped

In a large soup pot, combine the yellow peppers, onion, oil, salt, and black pepper. Cook over high heat for 8 to 10 minutes, or until the vegetables are tender. Add the broth, potato, and celery and bring to a boil. Reduce the heat to medium, cover, and cook for 12 to 15 minutes, or until the potato is tender. Carefully place half of the mixture at a time into a blender and purée until smooth. Serve immediately.

NOTE: When I'm feeling creative, I make half of this recipe with yellow bell peppers and half with red bell peppers. Then I swirl the two soups together in individual soup bowls.

Spinach-Potato Soup

8 to 10 servings

The lunch bunch flips for this soup, especially when it's paired with a hearty sandwich. When I serve this, "Fill 'em up and watch 'em go!" is the motto at my house!

2 tablespoons olive oil
3 medium-sized potatoes, diced
1 medium-sized onion,
   chopped
½ teaspoon minced garlic
2 cans (15½ ounces each)
   Great Northern beans,
   undrained

2 cans (10½ ounces each)
   condensed chicken broth
4 cups water
5 ounces fresh spinach,
   washed, trimmed, and
   chopped
½ teaspoon salt
½ teaspoon black pepper

In a large soup pot, heat the oil over medium-high heat. Add the potatoes, onion, and garlic and sauté for 4 to 5 minutes, or until the vegetables are tender. Mash 1 can of beans with a fork and add to the soup pot along with the remaining ingredients. Bring to a boil, then reduce the heat to medium and simmer for 30 minutes so the flavors can "marry," stirring occasionally.

NOTE: Mashing one can of the beans creates a thicker soup, but if you prefer a broth-type of soup, just add all the beans straight from the can, without mashing.

Spicy Sausage and Bean Soup

8 to 10 servings

You might not have thought of sausage as a soup ingredient, but once you try this, you'll think of it all the time!

1 teaspoon olive oil
1 pound bulk hot Italian
  sausage (see Note)
1 small onion, chopped
2 garlic cloves, minced
4 cans (15½ ounces each)
  Great Northern beans,
  undrained

2 cans (14½ ounces each)
  ready-to-use chicken broth
1 can (14½ ounces) diced
  tomatoes, undrained
1 teaspoon dried basil
½ teaspoon black pepper

In a large soup pot, heat the oil over medium-high heat. Add the sausage, onion, and garlic and cook for 5 to 6 minutes, or until no pink remains in the sausage, stirring frequently to break up the meat. Add the remaining ingredients and bring to a boil. Reduce the heat to medium-low and simmer, uncovered, for 30 minutes.

NOTE: I like this soup spicy, but if you prefer to use a mild sausage—or even turkey sausage—go ahead. Make it your own!

Creamy Tomato Soup

5 to 6 servings

No, tomato soup doesn't always come out of a can. And when it comes out of your kitchen, made from scratch . . . wow, what a scrumptious difference!

2 cans (28 ounces each) crushed tomatoes	½ teaspoon garlic powder
1 tablespoon sugar	1 teaspoon salt
1½ teaspoons dried basil	1 teaspoon black pepper
	2 cups (1 pint) heavy cream

In a large soup pot, combine all the ingredients except the heavy cream; bring to a boil over medium-high heat, stirring occasionally. Reduce the heat to low and slowly stir in the cream. Simmer for 4 to 5 minutes, or until heated through; do not allow to boil.

NOTE: Make sure to serve lots of crackers with this soup—I especially like oyster crackers in it.

Artichoke and Fennel Soup

4 to 5 servings

This combination of flavors is so fabulous, I could hardly believe my taste buds the first time I tried it! You've gotta taste it for yourself. . . .

2 tablespoons olive oil
1 fennel bulb, trimmed and coarsely chopped (see Note)
1 teaspoon minced garlic
2 cans (14½ ounces each) ready-to-use chicken broth

1 can (14 ounces) artichoke hearts, drained (liquid reserved) and chopped
½ cup heavy cream

In a large soup pot, heat the olive oil over medium heat. Sauté the fennel for 8 to 10 minutes, or until tender. Add the garlic and cook for 2 to 3 minutes, until golden. Stir in the chicken broth. Reduce the heat to low and simmer for 15 to 20 minutes. Add the artichoke hearts and reserved liquid; cook for 5 more minutes. Carefully place the soup in a blender or food processor in batches and purée until smooth. Return the soup to the pot and slowly stir in the cream. Simmer over low heat for 5 minutes; do not allow to boil. Serve immediately.

NOTE: Fennel bulbs can be found in the supermarket produce department at most times of the year. See page 231 for an explanation of how to trim a fennel bulb. Oh—a perfect way to use the feathery green leaves on top of the fennel bulb is to chop 2 to 3 tablespoons of them and add them to this soup for a splash of color. Garnish each serving with additional leaves, if desired.

Zucchini Cream Soup

4 to 6 servings

This one uses the "cream of the crop," 'cause garden-fresh zucchini and heavy cream turn out to be one "souper" combo!

2 tablespoons olive oil	2 teaspoons dried oregano
4 medium-sized zucchini, finely chopped	¾ teaspoon salt
	¼ teaspoon black pepper
1 small onion, finely chopped	3 tablespoons cornstarch
2 cans (14½ ounces each) ready-to-use chicken broth	¼ cup water
	1 cup (½ pint) heavy cream

In a large soup pot, heat the oil over medium-low heat. Add the zucchini and onion; cover and cook for 20 minutes, stirring occasionally. Add the broth, oregano, salt, and pepper. Cover and cook for 30 minutes. In a small bowl, whisk together the cornstarch and water until smooth and thoroughly combined. Increase the heat to medium-high and slowly stir the cornstarch mixture into the soup; continue to stir until the soup thickens. Reduce the heat to low and slowly stir in the cream. Simmer for 5 minutes; do not allow to boil. Serve immediately.

NOTE: If you want a totally smooth zucchini soup, before adding the cornstarch and water mixture, process the soup in a food processor or blender, then continue as above.

Breads and Pizza
Pane e Pizze

continued

NOTE: When working with pizza and bread dough, you may find it often becomes too sticky to handle. If that happens, simply dust your hands and work surface lightly with flour. That should take care of the stickiness so you can continue with your recipe!

My Favorite Italian Bread

1 loaf

When you "knead" something special that doesn't cost a lot of "dough," this one will surely "rise" to the occasion!

2¼ cups all-purpose flour, plus more if needed
1 package (¼ ounce) active dry yeast

2 teaspoons salt
1 cup very warm water
1 teaspoon sugar
2 teaspoons olive oil

Place the flour, yeast, and salt in a food processor that has been fitted with its metal cutting blade. Process for 3 to 5 seconds, until the ingredients are well mixed. In a small bowl, combine the water, sugar, and oil. With the processor running, slowly pour the water mixture through the feed tube. After it is completely mixed, if the dough is too soft, add more flour, 1 tablespoon at a time, until a smooth ball forms. Process for 20 to 25 seconds to knead the dough. Place the dough in a bowl that has been coated with nonstick cooking spray; turn the dough. Cover with plastic wrap and allow to rise at room temperature for 35 to 40 minutes, or until doubled in size. Punch down the dough, cover, and let sit for 10 minutes. Turn the dough onto a lightly floured board and roll out into a rectangle about 8″ × 12″. Starting at a long side, tightly roll up the dough jelly-roll fashion and place seam side down on an ungreased baking sheet. Cover with plastic wrap and let rise at room temperature for 30 minutes, or until doubled in size. Preheat the oven to 400°F. Remove the plastic wrap and bake for 30 to 35 minutes, or until golden brown. Let cool before slicing.

Spaghetti Sauce Bread

1 loaf

Who doesn't like dipping crusty bread into spaghetti sauce? Well, there's no dipping needed here 'cause the sauce is already baked in!

All-purpose flour for dusting
1 pound frozen bread dough,
   thawed
¼ cup (½ stick) butter, melted,
   divided

1 package (1¼ ounces) dry
   spaghetti sauce mix

Dust a work surface and rolling pin with flour. Roll the dough out to a 9″ × 18″ rectangle. Brush the dough with 3 tablespoons melted butter. Reserve 2 teaspoons of the spaghetti sauce mix, then sprinkle the remaining mix over the top of the dough. From a short end, tightly roll up the dough jelly-roll fashion and place seam side down in an ungreased 9″ × 5″ loaf pan. Brush the top with the remaining 1 tablespoon butter and sprinkle the reserved 2 teaspoons spaghetti sauce mix over the top. Cover loosely with plastic wrap and let rise in a warm place for 1 hour, or until doubled in size. Preheat the oven to 350°F. Remove the plastic wrap and bake for 30 to 35 minutes, or until golden. Let cool slightly before slicing.

NOTE: This is the perfect bread to go along with good old spaghetti and meatballs.

All-Around Beef Stromboli

1 loaf

Depending on how hungry the gang is, these hearty pockets make a super snack, a tempting appetizer, or a filling meal!

½ pound bulk hot or sweet Italian sausage
¼ pound ground beef
1 can (7 ounces) sliced mushrooms, drained
1 pound frozen bread dough, thawed

½ cup (2 ounces) shredded mozzarella cheese
1 teaspoon grated Parmesan cheese
½ teaspoon garlic powder
⅛ teaspoon salt
⅛ teaspoon black pepper

Preheat the oven to 425°F. In a large skillet, brown the sausage and ground beef for 8 to 10 minutes over medium-high heat, until no pink remains, stirring to break up the meat while cooking. Drain off the excess liquid and add the mushrooms; cook for 2 more minutes. Remove from the heat and allow to cool slightly. On a lightly floured surface, roll out the dough to a 6″ × 12″ rectangle. Spread the meat mixture onto the dough, leaving a ½-inch border around the edges. Sprinkle with the remaining ingredients, fold the dough over the filling, and, with your fingers or a fork, pinch the edges together firmly to seal. Place the stromboli on a baking sheet that has been coated with nonstick cooking spray. Bake for 15 to 18 minutes, or until the crust is golden brown. Slice and serve.

NOTE: I like to serve slices of this bread with some warmed marinara sauce—it practically makes a complete meal.

Mediterranean Biscuit Bread

12 to 16 servings

Bread always tastes better when it's pulled apart instead of sliced. It's so easy to tear off your share!

1 large package (17.3 ounces) refrigerated buttermilk biscuits (8 biscuits), each cut into sixths
1 small package (10.8 ounces) refrigerated buttermilk biscuits (5 biscuits), each cut into sixths

1 package (0.7 ounce) dry Italian dressing mix
1 tablespoon butter, melted

Preheat the oven to 325°F. Place the biscuit pieces in a large bowl and add the dry dressing mix. Toss until the biscuits are evenly coated. Add the melted butter and toss again. Place in a Bundt pan that has been coated with nonstick cooking spray. Bake for 30 to 35 minutes, or until golden brown on top. Let cool for 10 minutes, then remove from the pan. Serve warm or cool.

NOTE: For a cheesy bread, toss the biscuit pieces with 1 cup (4 ounces) shredded mozzarella, Cheddar, or other similar cheese after tossing them with the butter.

Sun-dried Tomato Bread

1 loaf

Surprisingly simple, this homemade bread will win you raves for originality!

1 pound frozen bread dough, thawed

½ cup sun-dried tomatoes in oil, drained (oil reserved) and chopped

1 tablespoon chopped fresh basil

1 tablespoon grated Parmesan cheese

On a lightly floured surface, roll out the dough to a 9" × 15" rectangle. Cover the entire surface evenly with the tomatoes, basil, and Parmesan cheese. Roll the dough up tightly jelly-roll style, starting at a short end. Brush the surface lightly with the reserved oil from the sun-dried tomatoes. Place the loaf seam side down in a 9" × 5" loaf pan that has been coated with non-stick cooking spray. Cover with plastic wrap and allow to rise for 1 hour, or until doubled in size. Preheat the oven to 375°F. Remove the plastic wrap and bake for 30 to 35 minutes, or until golden brown.

Easter Egg Bread Twist

1 loaf

What a great novelty bread! It's almost too pretty to eat—and so much fun to make. Why, you'll feel as "hoppy" as a kid! (Sorry— I couldn't resist!)

2 cups plus 2 teaspoons water, divided
4 teaspoons white vinegar
4 eggs (see Note)

4 different food colors
1 pound frozen bread dough, thawed
⅓ cup confectioners' sugar

In each of 4 cups or small bowls, combine ½ cup water and 1 teaspoon vinegar. Add about ¼ teaspoon of a different food color to each cup. Place 1 egg in each cup and allow to sit until the desired color is attained, turning the eggs occasionally with a spoon. Remove to paper towels to drain and dry completely. Divide the dough into thirds. On a lightly floured surface, roll

Let's twist again!

each piece of dough into a 24-inch rope. Braid the strips together and place on a baking sheet to form a ring, pinching the ends together to seal. Tuck the colored eggs into the braid, spacing them evenly. Cover loosely with plastic wrap and let rise at room temperature for 1 hour, or until doubled in size. Preheat the oven to 375°F. Bake for 25 to 30 minutes, or until golden brown. Allow to cool slightly. In a small bowl, combine the confectioners' sugar and the remaining 2 teaspoons water, stirring until thoroughly blended. Brush the warm bread with the sugar glaze, being careful not to coat the colored eggs. Serve warm, or cover and chill until ready to serve.

NOTE: Feel free to decorate the eggs any way you like, but remember they need to be raw when you start (so they don't overcook).

Florentine Bread Roll

2 loaves

Ahh, Florence—many say it's the most romantic of Italian cities. Well, I can't promise that this bread roll will improve your love life, but it could be the start of a very romantic dinner for two!

1 tablespoon olive oil
1 package (10 ounces) frozen
   chopped spinach, thawed
   and well drained
4 garlic cloves, minced
1 cup ricotta cheese

1 cup (4 ounces) shredded
   mozzarella cheese
½ teaspoon dried oregano
½ teaspoon salt
1 package (10 ounces)
   refrigerated pizza dough

Preheat the oven to 425°F. In a large skillet, heat the oil over medium-high heat. Add the spinach and garlic and sauté for 3 to 5 minutes, or until the garlic is golden. Remove from the heat and allow to cool slightly. In a large bowl, combine the ricotta and mozzarella cheeses, the oregano, and salt. Add the spinach mixture and stir until well blended. Unroll the pizza dough and, with your fingertips or the heels of your hands, spread the dough out to a 10″ × 15″ rectangle. Cut in half lengthwise to make two 5″ × 15″ rectangles. Spread half of the spinach mixture onto each piece of dough, leaving a ½-inch border around the edges. Fold each piece of dough over lengthwise and pinch the edges to seal securely. With a sharp knife, score the dough every 2 inches across the top and place on a baking sheet that has been coated with nonstick cooking spray. Bake for 10 to 12 minutes, or until golden brown.

Studded Italian Bread

1 loaf

Sometimes we want something just a little more hearty than a plain old piece of bread. This meaty loaf will fill you up—but you'll still be asking for more!

1 pound frozen bread dough, thawed
1 teaspoon olive oil
½ teaspoon garlic powder
⅛ teaspoon salt
¼ teaspoon black pepper

¼ pound assorted Italian cold cuts, chopped
15 slices pepperoni, chopped
¾ cup (3 ounces) shredded Italian cheese blend

On a lightly floured surface, slightly roll out or stretch the dough. Drizzle the oil over the top and sprinkle with the garlic powder, salt, and pepper. Scatter the remaining ingredients over the dough and knead until thoroughly combined. Shape into a round loaf and place on a large rimmed baking sheet. Cover with plastic wrap and allow to rise for 30 minutes, or until doubled in size. Preheat the oven to 400°F. Remove the plastic wrap and bake for 25 to 30 minutes, or until golden.

NOTE: Any type of cold cuts can be used. Try your choice of salami, ham, or a combination of both.

Twice-Baked Pepper-Fennel Crisps

about 24 crisps

Try saying this name three times fast . . . ! Whew! These are a lot like the bagel chips that are so popular. What makes them different? It's in the flavoring.

1 pound frozen bread dough, thawed
1 teaspoon cracked black pepper

1 teaspoon fennel seeds
1 teaspoon olive oil

On a lightly floured surface, flatten the dough slightly. Sprinkle the remaining ingredients over the top and knead until thoroughly combined. Place the dough in a bowl. Cover with plastic wrap and allow to rise at room temperature for 35 to 40 minutes, or until doubled in size. Cut the dough in half and roll each piece of dough into a long loaf. Place the loaves on a baking sheet that has been coated with nonstick cooking spray. Cover with plastic wrap and allow to rise again for 30 minutes, or until doubled in size. Preheat the oven to 400°F. Remove the plastic wrap and bake for 20 to 25 minutes, or until golden brown. Cool slightly and cut into 1-inch slices. (Leave the oven on.) Place cut side down on baking sheets and bake for 8 to 10 more minutes, or until golden and crisp.

NOTE: See the Note about cracked black pepper on page 15.

Sesame-Parmesan Bread Sticks

Bread sticks aren't hard to make—just a twist of the wrist and you'll be saying, "Gee, that was easy!"

¼ cup olive oil
6 tablespoons grated Parmesan
  cheese
¼ cup sesame seeds

1 pound prepared bread dough
  (see Note)
2 tablespoons all-purpose flour

Preheat the oven to 450°F. Pour the oil into a 9″ × 13″ baking dish. In another 9″ × 13″ baking dish, combine the cheese and sesame seeds; set aside. Divide the dough into 16 pieces and shape each piece into a ball. With lightly floured hands, roll each ball into a rope about 12 inches long. Dip each rope in the oil, then into the sesame seed mixture, coating evenly. Gently twist each rope several times to create a spiraled look, then lay the bread sticks about 2 inches apart on 2 baking sheets that have been coated with nonstick cooking spray. Bake for 10 to 12 minutes, or until crisp and golden brown.

NOTE: Fresh bread dough is usually available in the bakery section of the supermarket. If you don't see it, just ask.

Herb Focaccia

6 to 9 slices

If you haven't discovered this super change-of-pace bread, you're in for a real treat. There are many types of focaccia, and this one is simply baked pizza dough sprinkled with flavorful herbs. Sliced thick or thin, it's a favorite Italian go-along!

1 pound frozen bread dough,
   thawed
2 tablespoons olive oil
½ teaspoon dried oregano

½ teaspoon dried basil
½ teaspoon minced garlic
⅛ teaspoon salt

Preheat the oven to 450°F. Using your fingertips or the heels of your hands, spread the dough to cover the bottom of a 10″ × 15″ rimmed baking sheet that has been coated with nonstick cooking spray. Prick the dough 15 to 20 times with a fork and brush with the oil. In a small bowl, combine the remaining ingredients and sprinkle over the dough. Bake for 8 to 10 minutes, or until the focaccia is crisp and brown. Cut into slices and serve.

NOTE: If you want to use fresh herbs, use about three times as much of each. That means if ½ teaspoon dried herb is called for, you should use 1½ teaspoons chopped fresh herbs. Fresh herbs are widely available in the produce department of supermarkets.

Olive Focaccia

12 to 16 strips

Nothing says Italy like olives. And mixing green and black ones says it all.

1 pound frozen bread dough, thawed
1 teaspoon olive oil
½ cup chopped pitted Kalamata or other black olives

½ cup chopped pitted Sicilian or other green olives
2 tablespoons grated Parmesan cheese
½ teaspoon dried oregano

Preheat the oven to 450°F. Using your fingertips or the heels of your hands, spread the dough to cover the bottom of a 12- to 14-inch pizza pan that has been coated with nonstick cooking spray. Push the dough out to the edge of the pan, forming a rim. With a fork, prick the dough 15 to 20 times. Brush with the oil. Sprinkle the olives over the top of the dough, then top with the cheese and oregano. Bake for 12 to 15 minutes, or until the focaccia is crisp and brown. Cut in half, then cut each half into 6 to 8 strips for easy serving.

NOTE: Kalamata and Sicilian olives can usually be found at the deli counter in larger supermarkets, and sometimes you can even find them pitted. If not, make sure to cut the olives away from the pits before placing them on the dough.

Traditional Pizza Dough

1 pound dough

Sure, you can buy prepared pizza dough at the grocery store. But why not try making it at home for an extra-special pizza?

2¼ cups all-purpose flour, plus
   more if needed
1 package (¼ ounce) active dry
   yeast

1 teaspoon salt
1 cup very warm water
1 teaspoon sugar
2 teaspoons olive oil

Place the flour, yeast, and salt in a food processor that has been fitted with its metal cutting blade. Process for 3 to 5 seconds, until the ingredients are well mixed. In a small bowl, combine the water, sugar, and oil. With the processor running, slowly pour the water mixture through the feed tube. After it is completely mixed, if the dough is too soft, add more flour 1 tablespoon at a time until a smooth ball forms. Process for 20 to 25 seconds to knead the dough. Place the dough in a bowl that has been coated with nonstick cooking spray; turn the dough. Cover with plastic wrap and allow to rise at room temperature for 35 to 40 minutes, or until doubled in size. Punch the dough down, cover, and let sit for 10 minutes. Use immediately, or place in a resealable plastic storage bag and keep refrigerated for up to 2 days before using. The dough may also be frozen in the plastic

KNEADING DOUGH

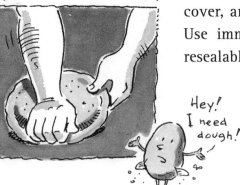

Hey! I need dough!

storage bag; just thaw overnight in the refrigerator, or at room temperature (out of direct sunlight) for 3 to 4 hours.

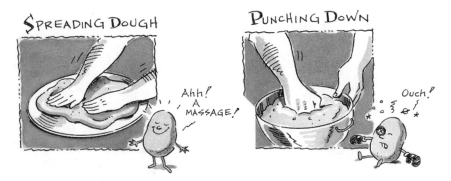

SPREADING DOUGH

Ahh! A MASSAGE!

PUNCHING DOWN

Ouch!

NOTE: No food processor? No problem. Just place the flour, yeast, and salt in a large bowl and mix until well blended. Slowly add the water mixture to the flour mixture, mixing until a crumbly dough forms. Turn out onto a lightly floured surface and knead for 4 to 5 minutes, or until the dough is satiny smooth and has an elastic feel. Add more flour, 1 tablespoon at a time, if necessary to achieve this consistency. Form into a ball and follow the directions opposite, starting with placing the dough in a bowl.

No-Rules Cheese Pizza

6 to 8 slices

Well, there really is *one* rule: Always make enough for seconds . . . and thirds!

1 pound pizza dough (page 76)
  or one 12- to 14-inch
  prepared pizza shell, thawed
  if frozen
¾ cup pizza or spaghetti sauce

¼ cup grated Parmesan cheese
1½ cups (6 ounces) shredded
  mozzarella cheese
½ teaspoon dried basil
½ teaspoon dried oregano

Preheat the oven to 450°F. If starting with pizza dough, using your fingertips or the heels of your hands, spread the dough out to cover the bottom of a 12- to 14-inch pizza pan that has been coated with nonstick cooking spray. With a fork, prick the dough 15 to 20 times. Brush with 1 teaspoon olive oil. If using a prepared pizza shell, place the shell on a pizza pan.

Spread the sauce evenly over the prepared pizza base. Top with the Parmesan cheese, then the mozzarella cheese. Sprinkle with the basil and oregano (and other favorite toppings, if desired—see next page) and bake for 10 to 11 minutes, or until the crust is crisp and brown. Cut and serve.

Toppings for Cheese Pizza

There are so many choices when it comes to customizing your own pizza! And this list should take all of the guesswork out of how much of various toppings you should need. These amounts are a guide for when you're using just one topping on a whole 12- to 14-inch pizza. If you want to mix and match, cut down the amount of each topping. For example, if you use two toppings, cut each one in half—or, if you use four toppings, use a quarter of the amount given for each, right? You've got it!

Extra Cheese: 1 (extra) cup (4 ounces), shredded

Pepperoni: 2 to 3 ounces, thinly sliced (about 35 slices)

Sausage: ½ pound, cooked and crumbled

Fresh Bell Pepper: 1 medium-sized, cut into ¼-inch strips

Roasted Peppers: 1 jar (7 ounces), drained, patted dry, and cut into chunks or ¼-inch strips

Fresh Mushrooms: 5 ounces, sliced (about 2 cups)

Canned Mushrooms: 1 can (7 ounces) sliced or stems and pieces, drained

Onion: 1 large, thinly sliced and lightly sautéed

Fresh Spinach: 5 ounces (½ of a 10-ounce bag), washed and trimmed

Chopped Frozen Spinach: 1 package (10 ounces), thawed and well drained

Broccoli: 3 cups fresh florets, steamed, or 3 cups frozen, thawed and drained

Black Olives: 1 can (2¼ ounces) sliced, drained (about ½ cup)

Salami: 3 ounces, thinly sliced

Anchovies: 2 cans (2 ounces each), drained

Mixed Baby Greens Pizza

8 slices

Ooh, these tender, sweet baby greens will have you wishing you'd made more than one pie! After all, it *is* both our salad *and* our pizza.

1 pound pizza dough, thawed if frozen
2 teaspoons olive oil
2 tablespoons grated Parmesan cheese
1 teaspoon Italian seasoning
1 package (4 ounces) mixed baby greens
½ cup balsamic vinaigrette dressing

Preheat the oven to 450°F. Using your fingertips or the heels of your hands, spread the dough to cover the bottom of a 12- to 14-inch pizza pan that has been coated with nonstick cooking spray. Push the dough out to the edge of the pan, forming a rim. With a fork, prick the dough 15 to 20 times. Brush with the oil and sprinkle with the Parmesan cheese and Italian seasoning. Bake for 12 to 15 minutes, or until the crust is crisp and golden brown. In a large bowl, combine the mixed greens with the dressing; spread evenly over the crust. Cut and serve warm.

NOTE: Mixed baby greens can usually be found in the packaged salad section of the supermarket produce department.

Garlic Pizza

8 slices

One bite of this will surely be enough to keep the vampires away. Too bad for them . . . but lucky for us, 'cause it's packed with flavor!

One 12- to 14-inch prepared
   pizza shell, thawed if frozen
2 tablespoons butter, melted
6 garlic cloves, chopped
   (see Note)
½ teaspoon salt

¼ cup grated Parmesan cheese
1 cup (4 ounces) shredded
   mozzarella cheese
1 tablespoon chopped fresh
   parsley

Preheat the oven to 450°F. Place the pizza shell on a pizza pan. In a small bowl, combine the butter, garlic, and salt; mix well. Brush the mixture evenly over the pizza shell, then top with the cheeses and parsley. Bake for 10 to 12 minutes, or until the crust is crisp and brown. Cut and serve.

NOTE: Chopped garlic can be found all ready to go in the produce section of your supermarket in small jars—boy, does that make it easy! For this recipe, simply use the equivalent of 6 garlic cloves.

Pesto and Artichoke Pizza

8 slices

Sure, it's a little rich, but it's also a lot special!

One 12- to 14-inch prepared
   pizza shell, thawed if frozen
¼ cup prepared pesto sauce
2 tablespoons grated Parmesan
   cheese
1 can (14 ounces) artichoke
   hearts, drained and
   quartered

1 can (2¼ ounces) sliced
   olives, drained
½ cup (2 ounces) shredded
   fontina cheese (see Note)

Preheat the oven to 400°F. Place the pizza shell on a pizza pan and spread evenly with the pesto sauce. Top with the Parmesan cheese, artichokes, and olives, then sprinkle with the fontina cheese. Bake for 12 to 15 minutes, or until the crust is crisp and brown. Cut and serve.

NOTE: Fontina cheese usually comes in blocks, so you'll probably need to shred it yourself with a grater. Or you could just use another type of cheese that comes already shredded—even a blend.

White Pizza

8 slices

When most people think of pizza, they assume it's got to have a tomato-based sauce on it. Well, that's not true. Take white pizza, for example. It's got three different cheeses, loads of great flavor . . . and *no* tomatoes or tomato sauce.

One 12- to 14-inch prepared
   pizza shell, thawed if frozen
1 cup (4 ounces) shredded
   mozzarella cheese, divided
1 cup ricotta cheese
⅓ cup grated Parmesan cheese

3 garlic cloves, chopped
½ teaspoon Italian seasoning
¼ teaspoon onion powder
¼ teaspoon salt
⅛ teaspoon white pepper

Preheat the oven to 450°F. Place the pizza shell on a pizza pan. In a medium-sized bowl, combine ¼ cup mozzarella cheese and all the remaining ingredients; mix well. Spread the mixture over the pizza shell and sprinkle with the remaining ¾ cup mozzarella cheese. Bake for 10 to 12 minutes, or until the crust is crisp and brown. Cut and serve.

NOTE: Sprinkle the baked pizza with chopped fresh parsley to add a burst of color.

Caramelized Onion Pizza

6 to 9 slices

No, this wouldn't be confused with candy, but the caramelized onions *are* incredibly sweet.

2 tablespoons butter
3 medium-sized onions, cut into ¼-inch slices
1 package (10 ounces) refrigerated pizza dough

1 teaspoon olive oil
¼ cup grated Parmesan cheese, divided
2 cups (8 ounces) shredded mozzarella cheese

In a large skillet, melt the butter over medium heat. Add the onions and cook for 20 to 25 minutes, or until golden brown, stirring frequently. Remove from the heat. Preheat the oven to 425°F. Using your fingertips or the heels of your hands, spread the dough to cover the bottom of a 10″ × 15″ rimmed baking sheet that has been coated with nonstick cooking spray. Push the dough out to the edge of the pan, forming a rim. With a fork, prick the dough 15 to 20 times. Brush with the oil. Sprinkle 2 tablespoons of the Parmesan cheese over the dough, then top with the mozzarella cheese. Spread the onions evenly over the cheese, then top with the remaining 2 tablespoons Parmesan cheese. Bake for 5 to 7 minutes, or until the crust is crisp and brown.

NOTE: Make sure to cook the onions until they're tender and browned. This pizza tastes best when the onions are done that way.

Anchovy Pizza

8 slices

You'll never say, "Hold the anchovies!" again after tasting this.

1 pound frozen bread dough, thawed
1 teaspoon olive oil
2 cans (2 ounces each) anchovies, rinsed and drained

1 cup pizza or spaghetti sauce
2 cups (8 ounces) shredded Italian cheese blend
¼ teaspoon dried oregano

Preheat the oven to 450°F. Using your fingertips or the heels of your hands, spread the dough to cover the bottom of a 12- to 14-inch pizza pan that has been coated with nonstick cooking spray. Push the dough out to the edge of the pan, forming a rim. With a fork, prick the dough 15 to 20 times. Brush with the oil. Chop 1 can of anchovies and combine with the sauce in a small bowl, then spread evenly over the dough. Sprinkle the cheese and oregano over the top, then arrange the remaining whole anchovies evenly over the pizza. Bake for 12 to 15 minutes, or until the crust is crisp and brown.

NOTE: This is a real anchovy lover's pizza—so if you want just a hint of anchovy flavor, leave out the can that's used in the sauce, but do place a few whole anchovies on top.

Pizza Margherita

No, it's not named after the drink; it's actually a classic traditional Italian pizza recipe that your whole gang will want to make part of their own tradition.

1 pound pizza dough, thawed
  if frozen
1 can (14½ ounces) whole
  tomatoes, drained and
  coarsely chopped
1 tablespoon chopped fresh
  basil

½ teaspoon dried oregano
½ teaspoon garlic powder
½ teaspoon salt
¼ teaspoon black pepper
¼ pound fresh mozzarella
  cheese, patted dry and sliced
  ⅛ inch thick

Preheat the oven to 450°F. Using your fingertips or the heels of your hands, spread the dough to cover the bottom of a 12- to 14-inch pizza pan that has been coated with nonstick cooking spray. Push the dough out to the edge of the pan, forming a rim. With a fork, prick the dough 15 to 20 times. In a small bowl, combine all the remaining ingredients except the mozzarella cheese; mix well. Spread the mixture evenly over the dough, then top with the mozzarella slices. Bake for 10 to 12 minutes, or until the crust is crisp and brown. Cut and serve.

Goat Cheese Pizza

8 slices

Have you seen this on menus at gourmet pizzerias and pricey restaurants? Well, it's time to give it a try. (Did they think we wouldn't find out how easy it is?!)

1 pound pizza dough, thawed
   if frozen
1 cup pizza or spaghetti sauce
⅓ cup sun-dried tomatoes in
   oil, drained and chopped

2 tablespoons chopped fresh
   basil
3 ounces goat cheese (see Note)

Preheat the oven to 450°F. Using your fingertips or the heels of your hands, spread the dough to cover the bottom of a 12- to 14-inch pizza pan that has been coated with nonstick cooking spray. Push the dough out to the edge of the pan, forming a rim. With a fork, prick the dough 15 to 20 times. In a small bowl, combine the pizza sauce, tomatoes, and basil. Spread the sauce mixture evenly over the dough and top with the cheese, crumbling the cheese into small pieces. Bake for 12 to 15 minutes, or until the crust is crisp and brown. Cut and serve.

NOTE: You can use more or less of the goat cheese, depending on how much you like it.

Spinach Calzones

4 calzones

One of my Italian friends says *calzone* means "trousers." Another says it just means "stuffed dough." I'd rather eat stuffed dough, wouldn't you? (Oh, well, whatever the name translates to, we can be sure it means a great hand-held meal.)

1 container (15 ounces) ricotta cheese
5 ounces frozen chopped spinach, thawed and well drained
1 tablespoon Italian seasoning
1 teaspoon onion powder
1 teaspoon garlic powder
⅛ teaspoon ground nutmeg
1½ teaspoons salt
¼ teaspoon black pepper
2 pounds pizza dough, thawed if frozen
4 teaspoons olive oil

Preheat the oven to 450°F. In a medium-sized bowl, combine the ricotta cheese, spinach, Italian seasoning, onion powder, garlic powder, nutmeg, salt, and pepper; mix until well blended, then set aside. Divide the dough into 4 equal-sized balls. On a lightly floured surface, spread each dough ball with your fingertips or the heels of your hands to make a 7- to 8-inch circle. Spread one quarter of the spinach mixture on each of the dough circles, covering only half of each one and leaving a ½-inch border. Fold the dough over the filling, forming half-moons. With your fingers or a fork, pinch or press the edges together firmly to seal. Place the calzones on 2 baking sheets that have been coated with nonstick cooking spray and brush the top of each with 1 teaspoon oil. Pierce the tops 3 or 4 times with a fork or knife. Bake for 15 to 18 minutes, or until the crust is golden brown. Serve whole or cut as desired.

Sauces

Salse Tutti

Ten-Minute Marinara Sauce

about 4 cups

Got a few minutes? That's all it takes to stir up this hearty to-mato sauce . . . 'cause there's no long cookin' here!

¼ cup olive oil
4 garlic cloves, coarsely
    chopped
1 cup water
1 can (28 ounces) crushed
    tomatoes

¾ cup chopped fresh parsley
1 teaspoon dried oregano
1 teaspoon garlic powder
1 teaspoon salt
1 teaspoon black pepper

In a large saucepan, heat the olive oil over medium-high heat; add the garlic and sauté until golden. Slowly add the water, then the tomatoes; stir in the remaining ingredients and bring to a rapid boil. Reduce the heat to medium and cook for 10 minutes, stirring occasionally.

NOTE: This sauce is so quick to make, there's no need to do it ahead of time. It makes enough for about a pound of pasta.

Home-Cooked Spaghetti Sauce

about 10 cups

A must in every Italian kitchen is a good tomato sauce. This one fits the bill, so I'm sure you'll be making it over and over again.

1 tablespoon olive oil
1 garlic clove, minced
1 medium-sized onion, finely chopped
1 medium-sized green bell pepper, finely chopped

3 cans (28 ounces each) crushed tomatoes
1 can (6 ounces) tomato paste
2 tablespoons sugar (optional)
1 tablespoon dried basil
½ teaspoon black pepper

In a large pot, heat the oil over medium-high heat. Add the garlic, onion, and green pepper and sauté for 2 to 3 minutes, or until the onion and pepper are tender, stirring frequently. Add the remaining ingredients and bring to a boil. Reduce the heat to low and simmer for 1 hour, or until the sauce thickens, stirring occasionally.

NOTE: For added flavor, add 2 teaspoons dried oregano along with the other ingredients. Since this makes a lot of sauce, be sure to refrigerate (for up to 1 week) or freeze any leftovers in airtight containers.

Bolognese Sauce

about 5 cups

Here's a classic meat sauce that comes from the same place that gave us that other classic: Bologna sausage. (And that's no baloney!)

1 pound ground beef
1 carrot, shredded
1 medium-sized onion,
   chopped
1 garlic clove, minced
2 cans (15 ounces each) tomato
   sauce

1 beef bouillon cube
1 teaspoon sugar
1 teaspoon dried basil
1 teaspoon dried oregano
½ teaspoon Italian seasoning

In a large pot, brown the beef over medium-high heat. Drain off the excess liquid and add the carrot, onion, and garlic. Cook for 4 to 5 minutes, or until the onion is tender, stirring occasionally. Add the remaining ingredients; cover and reduce the heat to low. Simmer for 20 minutes, allowing the flavors to "marry," stirring occasionally.

NOTE: Rigatoni Bolognese is one of my favorites! Maybe it's the way the meat sauce gets trapped inside the rigatoni that makes it so good. Just mix this sauce with about 1½ pounds cooked rigatoni for a meal that'll satisfy the heartiest of appetites.

Blender Pesto Sauce

about 1½ cups

Sounds fancy, doesn't it? But it's as easy as can be 'cause just a few ingredients make this a pasta-perfect alternative to tomato sauce!

2 cups lightly packed fresh
   basil leaves
1 cup olive oil
1 cup grated Parmesan cheese

2 garlic cloves
½ cup pine nuts or walnuts
½ teaspoon salt

Combine all the ingredients in a blender or a food processor that has been fitted with its metal cutting blade; blend until smooth. Store in the refrigerator, covered, until ready to use as desired.

NOTE: Yup, it's super on pasta (it makes enough to toss with about 1 pound), cooked chicken, and even on salads. But when you want a creamy pesto sauce, make Classic Alfredo Sauce (page 98) first, then stir in 2 to 3 tablespoons of this pesto sauce (or even a prepared one). Then get ready for great pesto flavor with creamy richness, too!

Parsley Pesto Sauce

about 1½ cups

No fresh basil? No problem, 'cause pesto made with parsley gives a nice refreshing taste to the sauce that's already so darned versatile.

2 cups lightly packed fresh
   parsley leaves
1 cup olive oil
1 cup grated Parmesan cheese

2 garlic cloves
½ cup walnuts
½ teaspoon salt

Combine all the ingredients in a blender or a food processor that has been fitted with its metal cutting blade; blend until smooth. Store in the refrigerator, covered, until ready to use as desired.

NOTE: For a nice change of pace, we can toss this with about 1 pound of our favorite pasta.

Puttanesca Sauce

about 7 cups

This is probably the most Italian of all sauces, since every ingredient is a Mediterranean favorite. (So is the taste!)

2 tablespoons olive oil
1 large onion, halved and
 thinly sliced
6 garlic cloves, coarsely
 chopped
2 cans (28 ounces each) whole
 tomatoes, undrained,
 coarsely chopped
1 tablespoon tomato paste
2 cans (2 ounces each)
 anchovies packed in oil,
 undrained, coarsely chopped

2 cans (2¼ ounces each) sliced
 black olives, drained
1 tablespoon capers, rinsed and
 drained
1 teaspoon dried basil
1 teaspoon dried oregano
¼ teaspoon crushed red pepper
¼ teaspoon black pepper

In a large pot, heat the oil over medium-high heat. Add the onion and garlic and cook for 6 to 8 minutes, or until the onion is tender. Add the remaining ingredients, reduce the heat to medium, and cook for 30 more minutes, allowing the flavors to "marry," stirring occasionally.

NOTE: Since this recipe makes so much sauce, make sure to place any leftovers in an airtight container and store in the refrigerator. It should last that way for up to a week, but for longer storage, freeze until ready to use.

Roasted Red Pepper Sauce

about 6 cups

Red, hot, and spicy! Just watch those die-hard "pasta-holics" dive into this one.

6 large red bell peppers, quartered
3 tablespoons olive oil, divided
1 tablespoon minced garlic
1 can (28 ounces) crushed tomatoes

¼ cup chopped fresh parsley
½ teaspoon crushed red pepper
½ teaspoon salt
¼ teaspoon black pepper

Preheat the oven to 450°F. In a medium-sized bowl, toss the bell peppers with 1 tablespoon olive oil until well coated. Place on a large rimmed baking sheet and roast for 25 to 30 minutes, or until tender. Place in the bowl of a food processor that has been fitted with its metal cutting blade; purée the peppers. In a large pot, heat the remaining 2 tablespoons olive oil over medium-low heat and sauté the garlic until golden. Add the remaining ingredients and bring to a boil, then add the puréed peppers. Reduce the heat to low and simmer for 30 minutes, allowing the flavors to "marry."

NOTE: There are a lot of different flavored dried pastas now available in our supermarkets. This sauce is especially good with tomato-basil pasta and chive-flavored pasta.

Classic Alfredo Sauce

about 2¾ cups

Who would have thought a classic could be this easy? Yup—four ingredients, one pan, a few minutes, and we're ready for some really good eatin'!

½ cup (1 stick) butter	½ teaspoon black pepper
2 cups (1 pint) heavy cream	1 cup grated Parmesan cheese

In a medium-sized saucepan, melt the butter over medium-low heat and stir in the cream and pepper. Continue stirring for 6 to 8 minutes, or until hot. Stir in the cheese until thoroughly mixed and cook for 3 to 5 minutes, or until thickened, stirring frequently. Serve immediately.

NOTE: I like to toss this with about 1 pound of pasta and top with additional Parmesan cheese. There's a reason Fettuccine Alfredo is a classic, you know—it's the perfect marriage of wide noodles with cream sauce. We can even use spinach-flavored fettuccine to get a nice contrast between the green pasta and the white sauce.

Summer Veggie Marinara Sauce

about 6 cups

When life gives us lemons, we have to make lemonade. And when our gardens give us fresh veggies, we know it's time to make a special veggie-packed marinara sauce.

¼ cup olive oil
1 medium-sized zucchini, diced
½ of a medium-sized sweet onion, diced
2 teaspoons minced garlic
2 cups vegetable or tomato juice

8 medium-sized plum tomatoes, chopped
2 teaspoons sugar
1 teaspoon dried basil
1 teaspoon salt
1 teaspoon black pepper

In a large saucepan, heat the oil over medium heat and sauté the zucchini, onion, and garlic for 8 to 10 minutes, or until tender. Add the remaining ingredients and stir until well combined. Reduce the heat to low and simmer for 15 minutes, allowing the flavors to "marry."

NOTE: If you've got extra sauce, be sure to store it in an airtight container in the refrigerator; it should be fine that way for up to a week.

White Garlic Sauce

about ¼ cup

In Italian, this sauce is called *aglio e olio,* and it means garlic and olive oil–that's it! It's the simplest of sauces, and one of the best. Oh–with a little grated Parmesan cheese sprinkled on top, it's even better!

3 tablespoons chopped garlic
½ teaspoon salt
⅔ cup olive oil, divided

¼ cup chopped fresh parsley
½ teaspoon black pepper

In a small saucepan, combine the garlic, salt, and 1 tablespoon oil; heat over low heat for 7 to 9 minutes, or until the garlic is just golden, stirring constantly. Add the remaining oil, the parsley, and pepper and heat through.

NOTE: This makes enough sauce for about 8 ounces of pasta, so make extra sauce if you need more pasta than that.

Tasty Anchovy Sauce

about 1½ cups

No fish stories here—you'll be reeling in new fans for the great taste of anchovies. And they'll gobble it down hook, line, and sinker!

½ cup (1 stick) butter
¼ cup vegetable oil
2 garlic cloves, chopped
¼ cup chopped fresh parsley
2 tablespoons chopped fresh basil or 1 tablespoon dried basil

2 tablespoons plain dry bread crumbs
3 tablespoons lemon juice
1 can (2 ounces) anchovies, undrained, chopped
½ cup sour cream

In a large skillet, heat the butter and oil over medium-low heat until the butter melts. Add the garlic and sauté until golden. Add the remaining ingredients except the sour cream and cook, stirring, until heated through. Remove from the heat and allow to cool slightly, then stir in the sour cream until thoroughly blended.

NOTE: This is a different type of sauce to serve over pasta. You can also use it as a topping for broiled fish, sautéed veal, or grilled chicken.

White Clam Sauce

about 2¾ cups

Lots of garlic and clams, with a splash of wine and lemon juice. Now, that's my kind of clam sauce!

4 tablespoons olive oil, divided
2 tablespoons minced garlic
2 cans (10 ounces each) baby clams, undrained
¼ cup dry white wine
2 teaspoons lemon juice
¼ cup chopped fresh parsley
1 teaspoon salt

In a medium-sized saucepan, heat 1 tablespoon oil over medium-low heat and cook the garlic for 1 to 2 minutes, until golden, stirring occasionally. Add the remaining ingredients and cook for 10 minutes, or until thoroughly heated.

NOTE: You can't miss when you serve this over 1 pound of linguine or your favorite pasta. And if you'd like it a little snappier, add ¼ teaspoon crushed red pepper to the sauce.

Red Clam Sauce

When they're "clam-oring" for super taste from the sea, here's the top tomato!

¼ cup olive oil
2 garlic cloves, minced
2 cans (10 ounces each) baby clams, drained and liquid reserved
1 can (28 ounces) whole Italian tomatoes, drained and chopped

2 tablespoons chopped fresh parsley
¼ teaspoon crushed red pepper
¼ teaspoon salt
⅛ teaspoon black pepper

In a medium-sized saucepan, heat the oil over medium-high heat. Sauté the garlic for 1 to 2 minutes, or until golden. Add the reserved clam juice, the tomatoes, parsley, crushed red pepper, salt, and black pepper; bring to a boil. Add the clams and return to a boil. Remove from the heat.

NOTE: Serve on about 1 pound of your favorite pasta.

Roasted Garlic

enough for 2 people as a bread spread

This one definitely has to be enjoyed by both you *and* your honey, especially if you're planning on getting close!

1 large garlic bulb
About 1 teaspoon olive oil

About ⅛ teaspoon coarse
(kosher) salt

Preheat the oven to 325°F. Cut the garlic bulb in half crosswise and place cut sides up on a piece of aluminum foil. Lightly sprinkle the cut sides with oil and salt. Put the 2 halves back together and wrap tightly in the foil. Bake for 1½ to 2 hours, until very soft, then open the warm bulb and squeeze out the soft garlic pulp to use as a spread in place of butter.

NOTE: Since this cooks for a while, I usually make it when I'm cooking a roast or something else in the oven for a long time at the same temperature. That way, I'm not using extra energy.

Red Wine Vinaigrette

about 1⅓ cups

This one whisks together in no time to lightly dress up a salad that's sure to command attention. And the red wine vinegar gives it such super, rich taste.

½ cup olive oil
½ cup red wine vinegar
¼ cup finely chopped fresh
   parsley
½ of a small onion, finely
   chopped

2 garlic cloves, minced
1½ teaspoons sugar
½ teaspoon salt
⅛ teaspoon black pepper

In a small bowl, combine all the ingredients and whisk well. Cover and chill overnight to allow the flavors to "marry" before serving.

NOTE: This dressing can also be used immediately; just make sure that the sugar has dissolved completely.

Balsamic Vinaigrette

about ¼ cup

All vinegar is *not* created equal. Uh-uh! But balsamic is an ideal addition to almost any salad dressing.

¼ cup balsamic vinegar
2 teaspoons Dijon-style
  mustard

½ teaspoon salt
¼ teaspoon black pepper
½ cup olive oil

In a small bowl, whisk together the vinegar and mustard. Add the salt and pepper. Pour in the olive oil very slowly, whisking constantly until well combined and creamy.

NOTE: In addition to serving this over your favorite mixed greens, try it over asparagus that has been steamed and chilled. . . . Yummy!

Light Caesar Dressing

about 2 cups

By substituting just a couple of light items in this recipe for the usual high-fat ones, we get all the great gusto of Caesar dressing but with a lot less fat.

1 cup light mayonnaise
¾ cup low-fat milk
1 tablespoon Dijon-style
   mustard
2 tablespoons lemon juice

½ cup grated Parmesan cheese
½ teaspoon garlic powder
½ teaspoon salt
½ teaspoon black pepper

In a medium-sized bowl, combine all the ingredients and whisk until smooth and creamy. Use immediately or store in the refrigerator in an airtight container until ready to use.

NOTE: Toss with your favorite salad greens or make a quick and light Caesar salad by tossing this dressing with torn romaine lettuce and croutons. (And you can make some quick croutons by cutting day-old bread into 1-inch cubes, tossing with some garlic powder, salt, and black pepper, and toasting in a 300°F. oven until golden brown.)

Tossed Pasta
Pasta Mista

continued

Caesar Pasta Primavera

4 to 6 servings

When we want to look dressed up, we can put on a bow tie, right? So now we get to put just the right "dressing" on our bow ties!

12 ounces bow tie pasta
2 tablespoons olive oil
¼ pound asparagus, cut into
    1½-inch pieces
¼ pound snow peas, trimmed
2 medium-sized carrots, thinly
    sliced
1 medium-sized yellow or red
    bell pepper, cut into 1-inch
    chunks

3 medium-sized plum
    tomatoes, cut into thin
    wedges
2 teaspoons minced garlic
1 can (14½ ounces) ready-to-
    use chicken broth
1 package (1.2 ounces) dry
    Caesar dressing mix
¼ cup grated Parmesan cheese

Cook the pasta according to the package directions and drain. Meanwhile, in a large skillet, heat the olive oil over medium heat and sauté the asparagus, snow peas, carrots, and bell pepper for 2 minutes. Stir in the tomatoes and garlic. In a small bowl, combine the chicken broth and dressing mix; pour over the vegetables and bring to a boil. Reduce the heat to low and simmer for 5 to 7 minutes, or until the vegetables are crisp-tender, stirring occasionally. In a large bowl, combine the hot pasta and the vegetable mixture; add the Parmesan cheese and toss until well coated. Serve immediately.

NOTE: In a hurry? You can always use a thawed 16-ounce package of frozen vegetables in place of the fresh vegetables and simmer just until warmed through. Now that's easy!

Mushroom-Broccoli Cavatelli

4 to 6 servings

I bet even former President Bush would eat broccoli if he tried it *this* way!

1 pound frozen cavatelli pasta	3 cups fresh broccoli florets
¾ cup (1½ sticks) butter	6 garlic cloves, minced
½ pound fresh mushrooms, sliced	¼ teaspoon salt
	½ teaspoon black pepper

Cook the cavatelli according to the package directions and drain. Meanwhile, in a large skillet, melt the butter over medium-high heat and add the remaining ingredients; sauté for 5 to 6 minutes, or until the broccoli is tender. Stir in the cavatelli and reduce the heat to low. Simmer for 4 to 5 minutes to allow the flavors to "marry."

NOTE: Just about any fresh vegetables can be cut up for this cavatelli, making it truly your own signature recipe.

Elbows and Beans

3 to 4 servings

Mamma mia! Here's an unbeatable combo that's practically a national food staple in Italy. It's sure to be a hit in your neighborhood, too!

¼ cup olive or vegetable oil
6 garlic cloves, coarsely
   chopped
1 can (14½ ounces) whole
   tomatoes, undrained,
   broken up
1 tablespoon dried oregano
1 teaspoon salt
1½ teaspoons black pepper
2 cans (15 ounces each)
   cannellini beans, undrained
½ cup chopped fresh parsley
1 package (8 ounces) elbow
   macaroni
¼ cup grated Parmesan cheese

In a large saucepan, heat the oil over medium-high heat; add the garlic and sauté until golden. Remove from the heat and allow to cool slightly to prevent splattering, then add the tomatoes, oregano, salt, and pepper. Return the pan to medium heat and cook for 10 minutes, stirring frequently. Add the cannellini beans and parsley and continue cooking for 10 more minutes, stirring frequently. Meanwhile, cook the macaroni according to the package directions and drain. Add the macaroni to the bean mixture along with the Parmesan cheese. Stir until thoroughly mixed, then serve immediately.

Rigatoni with Zucchini

Zucchini is versatile, and it really isn't hard to grow. I guess that's why so many of us grow it in our own gardens. Okay, the next time *you're* overloaded with it, do what we do . . . make rigatoni with zucchini!

1 pound rigatoni pasta
2 tablespoons olive oil
1 large zucchini, cut into
  ½-inch chunks
1 large onion, cut into ½-inch
  chunks
1 can (10¾ ounces) condensed
  cream of celery soup

½ cup milk
1 teaspoon dried basil
½ teaspoon salt
½ teaspoon black pepper
6 plum tomatoes, sliced

In a large pot, cook the rigatoni according to the package directions; drain and set aside in a colander. In the same pot, heat the oil over medium-high heat and sauté the zucchini and onion for 6 to 8 minutes, or until the zucchini is tender. Add the soup, milk, basil, salt, and pepper; mix until well combined and cook until heated through. Add the tomatoes and rigatoni and toss until well combined. Reduce the heat to low and cook for 4 to 5 minutes, or until the pasta is heated through. Serve immediately.

NOTE: One cooking and mixing pot makes for easy cleanup—and who doesn't like that?!

Angelic Pasta

4 to 6 servings

With a name like this, it's *got* to be heavenly!

1 pound angel hair pasta
  (capellini)
¼ cup olive oil
3 garlic cloves, minced
3 large tomatoes, diced
1 teaspoon dried basil
  (see Note)

1 teaspoon salt
½ teaspoon black pepper
¾ cup chicken broth
⅓ cup grated Parmesan cheese

Cook the pasta according to the package directions and drain. Meanwhile, heat the oil in a large skillet over medium-high heat. Add the garlic and cook for 1 minute. Add the tomatoes, basil, salt, and pepper; cook for 3 minutes. Add the chicken broth and mix just until hot. Place in a large bowl and add the hot pasta; add the Parmesan cheese and toss well. Serve immediately.

NOTE: If it's available, use 1 tablespoon chopped fresh basil in place of the dried.

Sicilian Linguine and Eggplant

4 to 6 servings

I have to confess that I haven't always loved eggplant . . . but when I tried it like this, I changed my mind! Try it on your gang.

1 pound linguine
⅔ cup olive oil, divided
2 small eggplant (about
   1 pound total), cut into
   ½-inch chunks
   (see Note)
¾ teaspoon garlic powder

½ teaspoon dried oregano
¾ teaspoon salt
½ teaspoon black pepper
4 plum tomatoes, chopped
2 tablespoons chopped fresh
   parsley

In a large pot, cook the linguine according to the package directions and drain. Place the linguine in a large bowl and toss with 2 tablespoons oil; set aside. In the same pot, heat the remaining oil over medium-high heat. Sauté the eggplant for 10 to 12 minutes, until lightly browned. Add the garlic powder, oregano, salt, and pepper and sauté for about 5 minutes more. Add the tomatoes, parsley, and linguine and toss gently until heated through. Serve immediately.

NOTE: If you prefer, go ahead and peel the eggplant before cutting them into chunks.

Pasta Caprese

4 to 6 servings

Salad Caprese, the classic salad of fresh mozzarella cheese, tomatoes, and basil, is now a classic pasta dish. (Oh, does that make me happy!)

¾ cup olive oil
¼ cup balsamic vinegar
4 garlic cloves, minced
¼ cup chopped fresh basil
¼ teaspoon crushed red pepper
¼ teaspoon salt
⅛ teaspoon black pepper
1 pound plum tomatoes,
    chopped

½ pound fresh mozzarella
    cheese, cut into ½-inch
    chunks
12 ounces wagon wheel pasta
    or other medium pasta shape

In a large bowl, combine the oil, vinegar, garlic, basil, red pepper, salt, and black pepper. Add the tomatoes and mozzarella cheese and toss until well coated. Allow to marinate at room temperature for at least 30 minutes. Cook the pasta according to the package directions; drain, then place in a large bowl. Add the tomato mixture and toss until well coated, allowing the cheese to melt slightly. Serve warm.

Rosebud's Farfalle alla Vodka

This recipe comes from one of my favorite Chicago restaurants. It's a true Italian specialty, and when you see how easy it is to make at home, I bet it'll be showing up on your table all the time! (Of course, I still like to join the folks at Rosebud and have their chefs make it for me when I visit Chicago!)

1 tablespoon olive oil
1 tablespoon chopped garlic
¼ cup vodka
1 can (28 ounces) whole tomatoes, undrained, coarsely chopped
12 ounces bow tie (farfalle) pasta

1 container (8 ounces) mascarpone cheese (see page xxi)
2 tablespoons coarsely chopped fresh basil
1 teaspoon salt
1 teaspoon black pepper

In a medium-sized saucepan, heat the oil over medium heat. Add the garlic and sauté for 1 to 2 minutes, just until browned. Add the vodka and the tomatoes with their juice and bring to a boil. Reduce the heat to low and simmer for 15 minutes. Meanwhile, cook the pasta according to the package directions. Drain, return the pasta to its cooking pot, and cover to keep warm. Add the remaining ingredients to the tomato mixture and stir until thoroughly combined and the cheese is melted. Pour over the pasta and stir until combined, rewarming over low heat if necessary. Serve immediately.

Ziti with Sun-dried Tomatoes

4 to 6 servings

Everywhere we turn these days it seems as if somebody's making something with sun-dried tomatoes. Well, we can be just as trendy and use sun-dried tomatoes to give this simple pasta toss just the right flair!

1 pound ziti pasta
¼ cup olive oil
2 garlic cloves, minced
½ cup sun-dried tomatoes in oil, drained and slivered (see Note)
1 can (14½ ounces) ready-to-use chicken broth

½ cup ricotta cheese
½ cup grated Parmesan cheese
½ teaspoon salt
1½ teaspoons black pepper
½ cup chopped fresh parsley

Cook the ziti according to the package directions and drain. Meanwhile, in a large skillet, heat the oil over medium heat and sauté the garlic for 1 minute. Add the sun-dried tomatoes and sauté for 1 to 2 minutes. Add the chicken broth and stir just until hot. In a large bowl, toss the hot ziti with the sauce and the remaining ingredients until well blended. Serve immediately.

NOTE: You can also use sun-dried tomatoes that aren't oil-packed; just make sure to reconstitute them according to the package directions.

Macaroni and Peas

Yeah, I know, the name sounds a lot like that really popular dish, but it sure is different. Wait till you try it—you may never go back to that "other" dish again.

1 pound elbow macaroni
1 jar (28 ounces) spaghetti
  sauce

2 cans (15 ounces each) peas,
  drained

In a large pot, cook the pasta according to the package directions; drain and set aside in a colander. In the same pot, combine the spaghetti sauce and peas; bring to a boil over medium-high heat. Reduce the heat to low and simmer for 2 to 3 minutes, or until the peas are heated through. Return the pasta to the pot and toss to coat. Heat for 2 to 3 more minutes, or until heated through. Serve immediately.

Fresh Tomato Linguine

4 to 6 servings

When you grow your own tomatoes, you're always looking for different ways to use them. This has got to be one of the best!

1 pound linguine
½ cup olive oil
3 garlic cloves, minced
1 tablespoon dried basil
½ teaspoon salt
½ teaspoon black pepper
½ cup chicken broth

4 large ripe tomatoes, diced (see Note)
4 cups (16 ounces) shredded mozzarella cheese
½ of a red bell pepper, diced
¼ cup grated Parmesan cheese

Cook the linguine according to the package directions and drain. Meanwhile, in a small saucepan, combine the oil, garlic, basil, salt, and pepper. Cook over low heat for 1 to 2 minutes, until the garlic is tender. Add the chicken broth and heat until warmed, stirring occasionally. In a large bowl, combine the tomatoes, mozzarella cheese, and the heated oil mixture. Add the warm linguine and the remaining ingredients and toss until well combined. Serve immediately.

NOTE: Make sure to use ripe tomatoes to get the most flavor—or even plum tomatoes, although you may need 6 to 8 of them, depending on their size.

Garlic Pasta

4 to 6 servings

Where would pasta—or any Italian meal—be without garlic? Not on my table, that's for sure. And here we get to feature it as the star attraction.

1 pound spiral or twist pasta
½ cup olive oil
6 garlic cloves, minced
½ cup finely chopped fresh parsley

1 teaspoon crushed red pepper
½ teaspoon salt
½ teaspoon black pepper
⅔ cup grated Parmesan cheese

Cook the pasta according to the package directions and drain; place in a large bowl and keep warm. Meanwhile, in a large skillet, heat the oil over medium-high heat; add the garlic and sauté until golden. Remove from the heat and mix in the parsley, red pepper, salt, and black pepper. Add the parsley mixture to the warm pasta, tossing until well coated. Add the Parmesan cheese and toss again. Serve immediately.

NOTE: This is a bit spicy; use less crushed red pepper if you want to cut back on the zip.

Family Gnocchi

4 to 6 servings

Be sure to have plenty of your favorite pasta sauce on hand when you serve these potato puffs. It's a meal with "a-peel"!

2 pounds potatoes, peeled and
   quartered
4 eggs

3 to 3½ cups all-purpose flour
2 teaspoons salt
½ teaspoon black pepper

Place the potatoes in a large pot and add just enough water to cover them. Bring to a boil over high heat, then reduce the heat to medium and cook for 20 to 25 minutes, or until the potatoes are fork-tender. Drain the potatoes and allow to cool to room temperature. Fill the large pot with water and bring to a boil over high heat. Place the cooled potatoes in a medium-sized bowl and mash with a fork. Add the eggs, 3 cups flour, the salt, and pepper; mix well. If necessary, add additional flour 1 teaspoon at a time until the mixture is firm enough to handle (and not sticky). Pinch off ½-inch pieces of the dough and place on a waxed paper–covered baking sheet. Carefully drop the gnocchi into the boiling water. Cook for 4 to 5 minutes, or until the gnocchi rise to the top and the centers are cooked through, stirring occasionally; drain and serve.

NOTE: Serve with Summer Veggie Marinara Sauce (page 99) or any of your favorite pasta sauces.

Chicken and Penne Pasta Toss

4 to 6 servings

The great thing about pasta is how versatile it is. All we have to do is toss in a few simple extras and it goes from ordinary to *extra*ordinary!

1 pound penne pasta
2 tablespoons olive oil
1½ pounds boneless, skinless
    chicken breasts, cut into
    ¼-inch strips
¼ cup (½ stick) butter
2 cups (1 pint) heavy cream
1 cup grated Parmesan cheese

1 teaspoon garlic powder
½ teaspoon salt
1 teaspoon black pepper
1 package (3 ounces) sun-dried
    tomatoes, reconstituted
    according to the package
    instructions and sliced

In a large pot, cook the pasta according to the package directions; drain and set aside in a colander. In the same pot, heat the oil over medium-high heat; add the chicken and sauté for 5 to 7 minutes, or until no pink remains. Meanwhile, in a large saucepan, combine the butter and heavy cream over medium heat. Bring to a boil, stirring occasionally, then reduce the heat to low and add the Parmesan cheese, garlic powder, salt, and pepper. Stir until smooth, then add the sun-dried tomatoes and heat through. Add to the chicken along with the pasta and heat over medium heat for 3 to 5 minutes, or until heated through and thoroughly combined, stirring constantly.

Chicken and Vegetable Orecchiette

4 to 6 servings

What's orecchiete? It's pasta that's shaped like a little bowl. Some people think it looks like a hat or an open shell. You can find it in most supermarkets in the pasta aisle, but if you can't find it, any small pasta can be used.

2 tablespoons olive oil
1 pound boneless, skinless
   chicken breasts, cut into
   ½-inch chunks
2 small yellow squash, cut into
   1-inch chunks
1 medium-sized zucchini, cut
   into 1-inch chunks

6 medium-sized plum
   tomatoes, cut into 1-inch
   chunks
1 teaspoon dried oregano
½ teaspoon dried basil
2 teaspoons salt
½ teaspoon black pepper
1 pound orecchiette pasta

In a large pot, heat the oil over medium heat and add the remaining ingredients except the pasta. Cook for 10 to 12 minutes, or until the vegetables are crisp-tender and the chicken is no longer pink, stirring occasionally. Meanwhile, cook the pasta according to the package directions and drain. Add the pasta to the vegetables and toss until well coated. Serve immediately.

NOTE: If you'd like, you can substitute a thawed and drained 16-ounce bag of frozen mixed vegetables for the squash and zucchini. Just add them when the chicken is almost cooked.

Rigatoni Mixed Pot

4 to 6 servings

Our meat-loving friends can't get enough of this dish. And neither can all those pasta lovers!

1 pound ground beef
1 pound hot Italian sausage,
   cut into 3-inch pieces
4 bone-in chicken breasts

2 jars (28 ounces each)
   spaghetti sauce
1 pound rigatoni pasta

In a large pot, brown the ground beef and sausage over medium-high heat, stirring to break up the beef. Drain off the excess liquid and add the chicken and spaghetti sauce; bring to a boil, stirring occasionally. Reduce the heat to low, cover, and simmer for 1½ hours, or until the chicken is completely cooked and tender. Cook the rigatoni according to the package directions and drain. Place the hot rigatoni in a large serving bowl and spoon the sauce and meats over the top. Toss lightly and serve.

NOTE: I usually remove the chicken from the pot, then toss the meats and sauce with the rigatoni to make sure the pasta is well coated. Then I just place the chicken on top and serve.

Pasta Bonanza

4 to 6 servings

I'm a big fan of one-dish pasta meals, and when I can have one that's as tasty as this, it's a real bonanza!

8 ounces elbow macaroni
1 tablespoon olive oil
1 pound ground beef
1 jar (28 ounces) spaghetti sauce
1 package (10 ounces) frozen mixed vegetables, thawed (see Note)

1 tablespoon onion powder
½ teaspoon garlic powder
½ teaspoon crushed red pepper
1 teaspoon salt

Cook the macaroni according to the package directions and drain; return to the pot and cover to keep warm. Meanwhile, in a large skillet, heat the oil over medium-high heat; add the ground beef and brown for 5 minutes, or until no pink remains, stirring to break up the meat as it cooks. Drain off the excess liquid, add the remaining ingredients, and reduce the heat to medium. Cook for 5 minutes, or until the vegetables are heated through. Pour the sauce mixture over the pasta and toss to coat; serve immediately.

NOTE: You can use all broccoli florets, or peas and carrots, instead of the mixed vegetables. For variety, make it with different veggies each time!

Cavatelli in Pepperoni Cream Sauce

4 to 6 servings

Eating out is always a treat, but sometimes we just want that same taste at home. Here's a no-fuss fancy that fits the bill!

1 pound frozen cavatelli pasta
2 cans (10¾ ounces each) condensed cream of celery soup
½ cup milk
2 medium-sized tomatoes, chopped

1 package (3 ounces) sliced pepperoni, each slice cut in half
2 teaspoons garlic powder
1 teaspoon dried thyme
½ teaspoon onion powder

In a large pot, cook the pasta according to the package directions; drain and set aside in a colander. In the same pot, combine the remaining ingredients and heat over medium-low heat for 10 to 12 minutes, or until bubbling. Return the pasta to the pot and toss to coat. Heat for 2 to 3 more minutes, or until heated through. Serve immediately.

NOTE: This is a great last-minute throw-together. The cavatelli is in the freezer, the soup is in the cupboard, the pepperoni is in the fridge, and the tomatoes are on the counter. In minutes, you've got a super meal.

Mostaccioli and Sausage

4 to 6 servings

Sounds pretty fancy, huh? Actually, mostaccioli pasta is simply a mustache-shaped tube pasta. You can use almost any shape, though, including penne, ziti, or shells, and this will still taste great.

1½ pounds hot or sweet Italian sausage, sliced about 1 inch thick
1 medium-sized onion, chopped
1 green bell pepper, chopped
2 jars (28 ounces each) spaghetti sauce
½ cup grated Parmesan cheese
1 pound mostaccioli pasta

In a large pot, brown the sausage over medium-high heat; drain off the excess liquid. Add the onion and green pepper; cook, stirring, until tender. Add the spaghetti sauce and Parmesan cheese. Bring to a boil, then reduce the heat to low, cover, and simmer for 15 minutes, stirring occasionally. Meanwhile, cook the pasta according to the package directions and drain. Toss the hot pasta with the sauce. Serve immediately.

Linguine with Mussels

4 to 6 servings

No muscle is needed to get the family to the table when this is served!

1 pound linguine
1 can (28 ounces) crushed
  tomatoes, undrained
1 pound fresh mussels, cleaned
  (see Note, page 40)
1 tablespoon dried parsley
  flakes

1 teaspoon dried oregano
1 teaspoon dried basil
½ teaspoon crushed red pepper
¼ teaspoon salt
¼ teaspoon black pepper

Cook the pasta according to the package directions and drain; place in a large serving bowl and cover to keep warm. Meanwhile, in a large saucepan, heat the crushed tomatoes over medium heat until simmering. Add the mussels and cook for 2 minutes. Stir in the remaining ingredients, except the pasta. Cover and simmer over low heat for 3 to 5 minutes, until the mussels open. **Discard any mussels that do not open.** Pour over the hot pasta and toss until evenly combined. Serve immediately.

Nice mussels, huh?

Cream Cheese and Lox Pasta

4 to 6 servings

I know cream cheese and lox doesn't sound very Italian, but this tastes so good I just had to include it. (After all, it *is* pasta!)

12 ounces bow tie pasta
1 cup milk
1 package (8 ounces) cream cheese, softened
1 tablespoon Parmesan cheese
¼ teaspoon onion powder

½ teaspoon salt
½ teaspoon black pepper
1 package (10 ounces) frozen peas, thawed
1 package (3 ounces) smoked salmon (lox), chopped

In a large pot, cook the pasta according to the package directions and drain; return it to the pot and set aside. Meanwhile, in a medium-sized saucepan, combine the milk, cream cheese, Parmesan cheese, onion powder, salt, and pepper over medium-low heat. Mix until the cheese is melted, then add the peas, reduce the heat to low, and simmer for 4 to 5 minutes, or until the sauce is warmed through. Add the salmon and the sauce to the pasta and cook over medium heat for 3 to 5 minutes, until thoroughly combined and warmed through. Serve immediately.

Homemade Crab Ravioli

6 to 8 servings

It's Chinese on the outside, Italian on the inside, and a favorite around the world!

2 cans (6 ounces each) lump crabmeat, drained
1 package (8 ounces) cream cheese, softened
½ cup ricotta cheese
2 tablespoons grated Parmesan cheese
½ cup chopped fresh parsley
2 scallions, finely chopped
½ teaspoon salt
½ teaspoon white pepper
4 packages (6 ounces each) wonton skins (about 64 skins total)

In a medium-sized bowl, combine all the ingredients except the wonton skins. Place a single wonton skin on a work surface and spoon a teaspoon of the crabmeat mixture onto the center of the wonton skin. Using a pastry brush or your fingertip, moisten the edges of the wonton skin with water. Fold one corner of the wonton skin over to meet the opposite corner, forming a triangle. Using your fingers, carefully seal the ravioli, being careful to keep the filling inside. Place on a large platter and repeat with the remaining ingredients. Meanwhile, bring a large pot of salted water to a boil over high heat. Place 12 ravioli in the boiling water and cook for 6 to 7 minutes, or until tender. Remove with a slotted spoon and place in a colander to drain completely. Continue with the remaining ravioli. Once all the ravioli are cooked, reheat as many as needed by placing in the boiling water for 1 to 2 minutes, until hot.

NOTE: Serve these topped either with warm marinara sauce or simply with grated Parmesan cheese.

Oven-Baked Specialties

Specialite al Forno

Baked Penne Primavera

6 to 8 servings

This one's an easy favorite of mine—fresh-from-the-garden taste with creamy fill-ya-up satisfaction.

1 pound penne pasta
1 can (10¾ ounces) condensed cream of asparagus soup
1¼ cups milk
1 package (0.7 ounce) dry Italian dressing mix
1 container (15 ounces) ricotta cheese

¾ cup grated Parmesan cheese, divided
2 packages (16 ounces each) frozen Italian mixed vegetables, thawed

Preheat the oven to 350°F. Cook the pasta according to the package directions and drain; set aside. Meanwhile, in a large bowl, combine the soup, milk, and dressing mix. Add the ricotta cheese and ½ cup Parmesan cheese; mix well. Add the cooked pasta and vegetables and toss until well coated. Spoon into a 9″ × 13″ baking dish that has been coated with nonstick cooking spray and sprinkle with the remaining ¼ cup Parmesan cheese. Bake for 45 to 50 minutes, or until heated through.

NOTE: There are a variety of different combinations of frozen Italian mixed vegetables. If you have other mixed vegetable favorites, use them; any one will do.

Stuffed Shells

6 to 8 servings

Here's an old restaurant favorite that's easier than ever to make at home.

12 ounces large pasta shells
1 container (32 ounces) ricotta cheese
3 cups (12 ounces) shredded mozzarella cheese, divided
½ cup plus 2 tablespoons grated Parmesan cheese, divided

2 eggs
1 tablespoon chopped fresh parsley
1 garlic clove, crushed
1 teaspoon salt
½ teaspoon black pepper
1 jar (28 ounces) spaghetti sauce

Preheat the oven to 350°F. Cook the pasta shells according to the package directions and drain. Meanwhile, in a large bowl, combine the ricotta cheese, 2 cups mozzarella cheese, ½ cup Parmesan cheese, the eggs, parsley, garlic, salt, and pepper; mix well. Spread 1 cup spaghetti sauce evenly over the bottom of a 9" × 13" baking dish that has been coated with nonstick cooking spray. Fill each shell generously with the cheese mixture, about 1 tablespoon per shell, and place the filled shells in the baking dish. Pour the remaining spaghetti sauce over the top. Sprinkle with the remaining 1 cup mozzarella cheese and 2 tablespoons Parmesan cheese. Cover with aluminum foil and bake for 40 minutes. Remove the foil and bake for 8 to 10 more minutes, or until the shells are heated through and the cheese is golden and bubbling. Let sit for 10 minutes before serving.

Baked Macaroni and Eggplant Neapolitan

6 to 8 servings

This one may be a mouthful to say, but every mouthful is a pure delight!

8 ounces ziti pasta
Olive oil for frying
1 medium-sized eggplant, peeled and thinly sliced
1 jar (28 ounces) spaghetti sauce, divided

2 cups (8 ounces) shredded mozzarella cheese, divided
⅓ cup grated Parmesan cheese, divided

Cook the ziti according to the package directions and drain. In a large skillet, heat ¼ inch of oil over medium heat until hot but not smoking. Cook the eggplant, a few slices at a time, until tender and well browned on each side, adding more oil as needed. Drain the eggplant on a paper towel–lined platter and cover to keep warm. Reserve 1 cup of the spaghetti sauce; combine the remaining sauce with the cooked ziti. Preheat the oven to 400°F. In a 9″ × 13″ baking dish that has been coated with nonstick cooking spray, layer half the ziti mixture, ¾ cup mozzarella cheese, half the eggplant, and 2 tablespoons Parmesan cheese; repeat the layers. Top with the reserved cup of spaghetti sauce, the remaining ½ cup mozzarella, and the remaining Parmesan cheese. Bake, uncovered, for 30 minutes, or until heated through.

NOTE: Make sure the eggplant is thinly sliced and cooked until very tender and well browned.

Four-Cheese Pasta

6 to 8 servings

Need a spur-of-the-moment dish for drop-ins? Well, nothing says Italy more than cheese, so the more cheese, the merrier the time!

2 tablespoons vegetable oil
1 small onion, finely chopped
2 cans (14½ ounces each)
    diced tomatoes, drained
1 teaspoon dried basil
½ teaspoon salt
½ teaspoon black pepper

½ pound ziti or bow tie pasta
1 cup ricotta cheese
4 slices (4 ounces) mozzarella
    cheese
4 slices (4 ounces) Swiss cheese
6 slices (6 ounces) provolone
    cheese

Preheat the oven to 350°F. In a large saucepan, heat the oil over medium-high heat. Add the onion, reduce the heat to low and cook, stirring occasionally, just until tender but not browned. Stir in the tomatoes, basil, salt, and pepper and cook for 10 minutes. Remove from the heat and set aside to cool slightly. Meanwhile, cook the pasta according to the package directions and drain. Spoon a thin layer of the tomato mixture over the bottom of a 9″ × 13″ baking dish that has been coated with nonstick cooking spray. On top of the tomato mixture, layer ⅓ of the pasta, all the ricotta cheese, the mozzarella cheese, another ⅓ of the pasta, all the Swiss cheese, and then the remaining pasta and tomato mixture. Top with the provolone cheese. Cover and bake for 30 minutes, or until the mixture is hot and bubbly. Let sit for 10 minutes before serving.

Baked Rigatoni

6 to 8 servings

Rigatoni doesn't have to be baked, but it just seems the natural way to cook it—especially because it doesn't "mush out" when you cook it this way.

8 ounces rigatoni pasta
1 container (15 ounces) ricotta
   cheese
3 cups (12 ounces) shredded
   mozzarella cheese, divided

1 can (4 ounces) sliced
   mushrooms, drained
1 jar (28 ounces) spaghetti
   sauce
½ cup grated Parmesan cheese

Preheat the oven to 350°F. Cook the rigatoni according to the package directions and drain. Place in a large bowl and add the ricotta cheese, 1½ cups mozzarella cheese, and the mushrooms; mix well. Coat a 9″ × 13″ baking dish with nonstick cooking spray and spread 1 cup of the spaghetti sauce evenly over the bottom of the dish. Spoon the rigatoni mixture over the sauce, then cover with the remaining sauce. Sprinkle with the Parmesan cheese and top with the remaining 1½ cups mozzarella cheese. Bake for 25 to 30 minutes, or until the rigatoni is heated through and the cheese is light golden.

NOTE: You might want to add a can of sliced black olives to the ricotta cheese mixture to give it a bit of zest.

Broccoli and Cheese Manicotti

4 to 6 servings

Not too long ago, only a chef would have attempted this dish. But nowadays, with so many prepared items available to us, we can all look like pros.

8 ounces manicotti shells	1 egg
1 container (32 ounces) ricotta cheese	¼ teaspoon salt
	¼ teaspoon black pepper
1 cup (4 ounces) shredded mozzarella cheese	1 package (10 ounces) frozen chopped broccoli, thawed and well drained
½ cup grated Parmesan cheese, divided	2 cups spaghetti sauce

Preheat the oven to 350°F. Cook the manicotti shells according to the package directions; drain, rinse, and drain again. In a large bowl, combine the ricotta and mozzarella cheeses, ¼ cup Parmesan cheese, the egg, salt, and pepper. Add the broccoli and mix well. Fill each manicotti shell with about ⅓ cup of the cheese mixture (see Note) and place them in a 9″ × 13″ baking dish that has been coated with nonstick cooking spray. Pour the spaghetti sauce over the shells and sprinkle with the remaining ¼ cup Parmesan cheese. Bake for 35 to 40 minutes, or until hot and bubbling.

NOTE: For an easy way to fill the manicotti shells, place the cheese mixture in a resealable plastic storage bag. Snip off a corner of the bag and squeeze the cheese mixture into the shells. For an extra burst of flavor, add ⅛ teaspoon ground nutmeg to the cheese mixture.

Eggplant Parmigiana

6 to 8 servings

Just what you'd expect—tender, tasty, and satisfaction guaranteed!

4 eggs
½ teaspoon salt
¼ teaspoon black pepper
2 cups Italian-flavored bread
    crumbs
About ¾ cup olive oil
2 medium-sized eggplant
    (about ¾ pound each), peeled
    and cut into ¼-inch slices

1 jar (28 ounces) spaghetti
    sauce
4 cups (16 ounces) shredded
    mozzarella cheese

Preheat the oven to 350°F. In a shallow dish, combine the eggs, salt, and pepper; beat well. Place the bread crumbs in another shallow dish. In a large skillet, heat 3 tablespoons oil over medium heat until hot but not smoking. Meanwhile, dip the eggplant slices in the egg mixture, then coat completely with the bread crumbs. Place the coated eggplant slices in the skillet a few at a time and cook for 2 to 3 minutes per side, until golden, adding more oil as needed. Drain on a paper towel–lined platter. Spread 1 cup spaghetti sauce evenly over the bottom of a 9″ × 13″ baking dish that has been coated with nonstick cooking spray. Layer half of the cooked eggplant evenly over the sauce, overlapping as necessary. Cover the eggplant with half of the remaining spaghetti sauce and top with 2 cups cheese. Repeat the layers, ending with the remaining 2 cups cheese. Cover with aluminum foil and bake for 45 to 50 minutes, or until hot and bubbly. Let sit for about 10 minutes before serving.

Zippy Spinach Fettuccine

6 to 8 servings

Okay, so salsa isn't Italian. It just thinks it is when it becomes part of this classic.

1 pound spinach fettuccine
1 tablespoon vegetable oil
1 medium-sized yellow squash, cut into 1-inch chunks
1 large red bell pepper, cut into 1-inch chunks
1 jar (28 ounces) spaghetti sauce
1 cup salsa (see Note)
1 cup (4 ounces) shredded mozzarella cheese

Preheat the oven to 350°F. Cook the fettuccine according to the package directions and drain. Meanwhile, heat the oil in a large pot over medium-low heat; add the squash and bell pepper and sauté for 8 to 10 minutes, or until tender, stirring frequently. Stir in the spaghetti sauce and salsa, then add the fettuccine; mix well. Place in a 9″ × 13″ baking dish that has been coated with nonstick cooking spray. Top with the mozzarella cheese and bake for 25 to 30 minutes, or until the fettuccine is heated through and the cheese is melted.

NOTE: Spicy or not spicy—it all depends on the "temperature" of the salsa you use. Just to keep it safe, I usually use a medium salsa.

Alfredo Pasta Twist

6 to 8 servings

We all love pasta, and when we come up with a new twist on an old favorite . . . Who could ask for more?

1 pound twist pasta	1 teaspoon salt
⅓ cup butter	½ teaspoon black pepper
3 tablespoons all-purpose flour	¼ cup grated Parmesan cheese
3 cups (1½ pints) heavy cream	½ cup Italian-flavored bread
2 cups (8 ounces) shredded	crumbs
Italian cheese blend	

Preheat the oven to 325°F. In a large pot, cook the pasta according to the package directions and drain; return it to the pot. Melt the butter in a large skillet over medium heat, stirring frequently. Add the flour and stir constantly for 1 to 2 minutes, or until the mixture is smooth and lightly browned. Stir in the cream and remove from the heat. Add the Italian cheese blend, salt, and pepper; mix well. Pour over the cooked pasta and toss to coat. Place in a 9″ × 13″ baking dish that has been coated with non-stick cooking spray. Sprinkle with the Parmesan cheese and then the bread crumbs. Bake for 30 to 35 minutes, or until heated through. Serve immediately.

NOTE: I like to add ½ teaspoon ground nutmeg to the cream mixture for some added flavor. (But I do that only when I'm sure that everybody I'm cooking for likes the flavor of nutmeg.)

Pepperoni Lasagna Pizza

6 to 8 servings

Two favorites rolled into one—what could be better?

12 lasagna noodles
4 cups (16 ounces) shredded mozzarella cheese, divided
1 package (3 ounces) sliced pepperoni
¼ pound fresh mushrooms, sliced
2 cups spaghetti sauce
1½ teaspoons Italian seasoning
⅛ teaspoon crushed red pepper

Preheat the oven to 375°F. Cook the noodles according to the package directions and drain; pat dry with paper towels. Place 6 noodles crosswise on a 10″ × 15″ rimmed baking sheet that has been coated with nonstick cooking spray, cutting the noodles to fit if necessary. Sprinkle 2 cups cheese over the noodles. Layer the pepperoni and mushrooms over the cheese. Cover with 6 more noodles placed in the same crosswise direction. Spread the sauce over the noodles, cover with the remaining 2 cups cheese, and sprinkle with the Italian seasoning and crushed red pepper. Coat one side of a large piece of aluminum foil with nonstick cooking spray and cover the pan with the coated side toward the lasagna (so the cheese won't stick); bake for 20 to 25 minutes, or until the pasta is heated through and the cheese is melted.

NOTE: For added flavor, sauté the mushrooms in a little butter before using.

Angel Hair Pie

4 to 6 servings

Pie for dinner?! Wow! You can be sure that this will be as big a favorite at your house as it is at mine.

8 ounces angel hair pasta (capellini)
2 tablespoons olive oil
2 eggs, well beaten
½ cup plus 2 tablespoons grated Parmesan cheese, divided

1 cup ricotta cheese
½ cup spaghetti sauce
½ cup salsa
½ cup (2 ounces) shredded Italian cheese blend

Preheat the oven to 350°F. Cook the pasta according to the package directions and drain. In a large bowl, toss the hot pasta with the oil. In a small bowl, combine the eggs and ½ cup Parmesan cheese; stir into the pasta. Pour the pasta mixture into a 9-inch deep-dish pie plate that has been coated with nonstick cooking spray and spread it over the bottom and up the sides to form a crust. Spread the ricotta cheese evenly over the crust, but not quite to the edge. In a small bowl, combine the spaghetti sauce and salsa; spread over the ricotta cheese. Bake, uncovered, for 25 minutes. Top with the shredded cheese. Bake for 5 more minutes, or until the cheese is melted. Remove from the oven and sprinkle with the remaining 2 tablespoons Parmesan cheese. Cool for 10 minutes before cutting into wedges.

NOTE: This is the perfect dish to make when you have leftover angel hair—it saves you a step and you get to make a completely new meal from leftovers.

Villa Valenti's Eggplant Rollatini

4 to 6 servings

I've enjoyed eating this dish at my favorite Italian restaurant in my hometown for more years than I can tell you. And Emma Valenti sure was gracious about sharing her recipe with me . . . for you.

4 eggs
1 teaspoon salt, divided
1 teaspoon black pepper, divided
2 cups Italian-flavored bread crumbs
2 medium-sized eggplant, peeled and cut lengthwise into ⅛-inch-thick slices (about 16 slices total)
About ½ cup olive oil

1 jar (28 ounces) spaghetti sauce, divided
1 container (32 ounces) ricotta cheese
2 cups (8 ounces) shredded mozzarella cheese, divided
¼ cup grated Parmesan cheese
1 teaspoon garlic powder

Preheat the oven to 350°F. Place the eggs, ½ teaspoon salt, and ½ teaspoon pepper in a shallow dish; beat well. Place the bread crumbs in another shallow dish. Dip the eggplant slices in the egg mixture, then coat completely with the bread crumbs. Heat 2 tablespoons oil in a large skillet over medium-high heat. Place the coated eggplant slices in the skillet a few at a time and cook for 2 to 3 minutes per side, until golden, adding more oil as needed. Drain on a paper towel–lined platter. Reserve 1 cup of the spaghetti sauce and pour the remaining sauce over the bottom of a 9" × 13" baking dish. In a large bowl, combine the ricotta cheese, 1 cup mozzarella cheese, the Parmesan cheese, garlic powder, and the remaining ½ teaspoon each salt and pepper; mix well. Place the cooked eggplant on a work surface and spread ¼ cup of the ricotta cheese mixture over the top of each. Roll up jelly-roll fashion and place seam side down in the baking dish. Pour the reserved 1 cup spaghetti sauce over the eggplant rolls and top with the remaining 1 cup mozzarella cheese. Bake for 35 to 40 minutes, or until the sauce is hot and bubbly and the cheese is melted.

Worth-the-Wait Lasagna

6 to 8 servings

One whiff of this and they'll hardly be able to contain themselves till it's done. It's a good thing we whipped up an antipasto to hold them over!

12 uncooked lasagna noodles
1 pound bulk hot Italian
   sausage
4 cups (16 ounces) shredded
   mozzarella cheese, divided
1 container (15 ounces) ricotta
   cheese

⅓ cup grated Parmesan cheese
1 egg
½ teaspoon dried basil
½ teaspoon black pepper
2 jars (28 ounces each)
   spaghetti sauce

Preheat the oven to 375°F. Cook the lasagna noodles according to the package directions and drain. In a large skillet, cook the sausage over medium-high heat until no pink remains, stirring to break up the sausage as it cooks. Drain off the excess liquid and set aside in a large bowl to cool slightly. Add 3 cups mozzarella cheese, the ricotta and Parmesan cheeses, the egg, basil, and pepper; mix well. Coat a 9″ × 13″ baking dish with nonstick cooking spray. Spread 1 cup spaghetti sauce evenly over the bottom of the dish. Place 3 noodles over the sauce. Sprinkle one third of the cheese mixture over the noodles. Pour 1 cup spaghetti sauce over the cheese mixture. Place 3 more noodles over the top and press down lightly. Repeat with 2 more layers of the cheese mixture, sauce, and noodles. Spoon the remaining sauce over the top and cover tightly with aluminum foil. Bake for 1 hour. Remove the foil and sprinkle the remaining 1 cup mozzarella cheese over the top; return to the oven for 5 minutes, or until the cheese has melted. Remove from the oven and allow to sit for 10 to 15 minutes before cutting and serving.

Baked Ravioli and Sausage

6 to 8 servings

Everything you always wanted in a plate of ravioli, and much more.

1 pound bulk hot Italian
  sausage
2 jars (28 ounces each)
  spaghetti sauce
1 package (25 ounces) frozen
  or refrigerated cheese ravioli
  (see Note)

1 can (7 ounces) sliced
  mushrooms, drained
1 cup (4 ounces) shredded
  mozzarella cheese

Preheat the oven to 350°F. Brown the sausage in a large skillet over medium-high heat for 8 to 10 minutes, until no pink remains, stirring to break up the sausage as it cooks. Drain off the excess liquid and place the sausage in a large bowl. Add the spaghetti sauce, ravioli, and mushrooms; mix well. Place in a 9" × 13" baking dish that has been coated with nonstick cooking spray and sprinkle with the cheese. Cover tightly with foil and bake for 45 minutes. Remove the foil and bake for 5 to 10 more minutes, or until the ravioli is heated through and the cheese is golden.

NOTE: If you thaw the frozen ravioli, or use refrigerated ravioli, the cooking time can be reduced by about 10 minutes.

Beefed-up Broccoli Lasagna

Remember when making lasagna was a day-long project, reserved for special occasions only? Try it this way, and I bet you'll change your mind.

1 pound lean ground beef
1 jar (28 ounces) spaghetti sauce
1 can (14½ ounces) Italian-style diced tomatoes, undrained
¼ teaspoon salt
1 package (10 ounces) frozen chopped broccoli, thawed and well drained

1 container (15 ounces) ricotta cheese
¼ cup grated Parmesan cheese
1 egg
10 uncooked lasagna noodles
1½ cups (6 ounces) shredded mozzarella cheese

Preheat the oven to 375°F. In a large skillet, brown the ground beef over medium heat for 8 to 10 minutes, until no pink remains, stirring to break up the ground beef as it cooks. Drain off the excess liquid. Add the spaghetti sauce, tomatoes, and salt; stir until well blended, then set aside. In a medium-sized bowl, combine the broccoli, the ricotta and Parmesan cheeses, and the egg; mix well. Spread 2 cups of the sauce mixture over the bottom of a 9″ × 13″ baking dish that has been coated with non-stick cooking spray. Press 4 noodles lengthwise over the sauce and 1 noodle crosswise across the end of the baking dish, completely covering the sauce mixture. Spread the ricotta mixture evenly over the noodles, then sprinkle with 1 cup mozzarella cheese. Top with 1½ cups of the sauce mixture, then arrange the remaining noodles over the sauce, pressing lightly into the sauce. Spread the remaining sauce over the top. Bake for 45 minutes, or until the noodles are tender. Remove from the oven and sprinkle with the remaining ½ cup mozzarella; cover with aluminum foil. Let sit for 15 minutes, then cut and serve.

Ravioli and Capicolla Pie

3 to 4 servings

When you hear that something's "easy as pie," you probably don't think of ravioli and capicolla pie. But wait'll you see how fast this perky pocket pasta bakes up into a hearty one-pan main dish.

1 package (20 ounces) frozen
   cheese ravioli (see Note)
½ cup prepared pesto sauce
1 jar (2 ounces) roasted peppers
¼ cup grated Parmesan cheese
¼ pound thickly sliced
   capicolla, coarsely chopped

½ cup (2 ounces) shredded
   mozzarella cheese
1 tablespoon grated Parmesan
   cheese

Preheat the oven to 350°F. Cook the ravioli according to the package directions and drain. In a large bowl, combine the pesto, peppers, Parmesan cheese, and capicolla. Add the ravioli and toss until evenly coated. Place in a 9-inch deep-dish pie plate and top with the mozzarella cheese. Cover loosely with aluminum foil and bake for 20 to 25 minutes, or until the ravioli is heated through and the cheese is golden. Top with the Parmesan cheese just before serving.

NOTE: Any type of ravioli can be used—fresh or frozen, filled with meat, vegetables, or cheese blends.

Eggplant Lasagna

True Italian taste and style are in every inviting morsel of this robust dish!

2 tablespoons olive oil
2 large onions, chopped
2 medium-sized eggplant, peeled and cut into ½-inch cubes
1 pound ground beef
2½ teaspoons salt, divided
¾ teaspoon black pepper

1 container (15 ounces) ricotta cheese
½ cup grated Parmesan cheese
2 eggs
1 teaspoon dried basil
1 jar (28 ounces) spaghetti sauce
2 cups (8 ounces) shredded mozzarella cheese

Preheat the oven to 350°F. In a large pot, heat the oil over medium heat and sauté the onions for 3 to 4 minutes, or until tender. Add the eggplant, cover, and cook for 10 to 12 minutes, or until tender, stirring frequently. Stir in the ground beef, 1½ teaspoons salt, and ¼ teaspoon pepper; cook, uncovered, for 6 to 8 minutes, until no pink remains in the meat, stirring to break up the meat as it cooks. In a large bowl, combine the ricotta and Parmesan cheeses, the eggs, basil, and the remaining 1 teaspoon salt and ½ teaspoon pepper; mix well. Coat a 9″ × 13″ baking dish with nonstick cooking spray and spread ⅓ of the spaghetti sauce evenly over the bottom of the dish. Spread ⅓ of the eggplant mixture over the sauce, then top with ⅓ of the cheese mixture and sprinkle with ⅓ of the mozzarella cheese. Repeat the layers 2 more times, ending with mozzarella cheese. Cover with aluminum foil and bake for 1 hour. Remove the foil and bake for 10 to 15 more minutes, or until the lasagna is heated through and the cheese is golden. Let sit for 10 minutes before serving.

Poultry
Pollame

continued

Chicken Alfredo

6 servings

Talk about temptation . . . ! Who could resist this creamy flavor combo?

2 eggs, lightly beaten
1 cup Italian-flavored bread crumbs
3 tablespoons olive oil
6 boneless, skinless chicken breast halves (1½ to 2 pounds total)
6 slices (6 ounces) mozzarella cheese (see Note)

2 cups (1 pint) heavy cream
1 cup grated Parmesan cheese
2 tablespoons chopped fresh parsley
½ teaspoon salt
¾ teaspoon black pepper

Preheat the oven to 350°F. Place the eggs in a shallow dish. Place the bread crumbs in another shallow dish. In a large skillet, heat the oil over medium-high heat until hot but not smoking. Meanwhile, dip the chicken breasts in the eggs, then in the bread crumbs, coating completely. Place half the chicken at a time in the hot oil and cook for 6 to 8 minutes, or until lightly browned, turning halfway through the cooking. Remove the chicken breasts to a 9″ × 13″ baking dish that has been coated with nonstick cooking spray. Top each breast with a slice of mozzarella cheese. In a medium-sized saucepan, combine the cream, Parmesan cheese, parsley, salt, and pepper and simmer over medium heat for 3 to 5 minutes, or until the mixture has thickened. Pour over the chicken and bake for 20 to 25 minutes, or until the chicken is cooked through and the cheese is light golden.

NOTE: Instead of mozzarella slices, you can use 1½ cups shredded mozzarella cheese or an Italian cheese blend; sprinkle it evenly over the chicken.

Shortcut Chicken Cacciatore

3 to 4 servings

It's the end result that counts when it comes to a great meal. Here's one that I know is sure to please . . . and it cooks up in a flash!

⅓ cup olive oil
2 medium-sized bell peppers (1 red and 1 green), thinly sliced
1 large onion, cut in half, then into ¼-inch slices
½ pound fresh mushrooms, sliced

One 3- to 3½-pound chicken, cut into 8 pieces
1 jar (28 ounces) spaghetti sauce
½ cup water

In a large pot, heat the oil over medium-high heat. Sauté the bell peppers, onion, and mushrooms for 3 to 4 minutes, or just until tender. Remove the vegetables to a medium-sized bowl, leaving any remaining oil in the pot. In the same pot, sauté the chicken pieces for 8 to 10 minutes over medium-high heat, until lightly browned, turning halfway through the cooking. Return the sautéed vegetables to the pot, then add the spaghetti sauce and water; mix well. Reduce the heat to medium-low, cover loosely, and cook for 30 to 40 minutes, or until the chicken is tender and cooked through.

NOTE: I like to serve cooked pasta with this chicken. That way, I can enjoy every last bit of the cacciatore sauce.

Classic Chicken Parmigiana

6 servings

This is one of my true Italian favorites. It's perfect for dinner, served up with some pasta and sauce, and it's great filling crusty Italian bread for an unbeatable sandwich, too.

2 eggs
½ teaspoon salt
¼ teaspoon black pepper
1½ cups Italian-flavored bread crumbs
6 boneless, skinless chicken breast halves (1½ to 2 pounds total), pounded to ¼-inch thickness

½ cup olive oil
1½ cups spaghetti sauce, warmed
2 cups (8 ounces) shredded mozzarella cheese

Preheat the oven to 400°F. In a shallow dish, beat together the eggs, salt, and pepper. Place the bread crumbs in another shallow dish. Dip each chicken breast into the egg mixture and then into the bread crumbs, coating completely; set aside. Meanwhile, in a large skillet, heat the oil over medium-high heat until hot but not smoking. Brown the chicken breasts 2 at a time for 2 to 3 minutes per side. Drain on paper towels. Place the browned chicken on a rimmed baking sheet that has been coated with nonstick cooking spray and spread the spaghetti sauce evenly over each piece. Sprinkle with the cheese and bake for 3 to 5 minutes, or until the chicken is heated through and the cheese is melted.

Three-Pepper Chicken

4 to 6 servings

Bold color and even bolder spices take baked chicken to new heights, along with your reputation as a kitchen whiz!

3 medium-sized bell peppers
   (1 red, 1 green, and 1 yellow),
   cut into strips (see Note)
2 tablespoons olive oil
2 teaspoons dried oregano
2 teaspoons dried thyme
2 teaspoons garlic powder

2 teaspoons onion powder
1 teaspoon paprika
¼ teaspoon crushed red pepper
1 teaspoon salt
One 3- to 3½-pound chicken,
   cut into 8 pieces

Preheat the oven to 350°F. In a large bowl, combine all the ingredients except the chicken; mix until thoroughly combined. Add the chicken and turn to coat completely. Transfer to an ungreased 9″ × 13″ baking dish and bake for 60 to 70 minutes, or until no pink remains in the chicken and the juices run clear.

NOTE: Any color bell peppers will work—I just like to use one of each color to make this a really bright dish.

Chicken with Capers

What *are* capers, anyway? They're the buds of a shrub that grows in the Mediterranean that are pickled and used for garnish *and* seasoning. They give dishes a unique taste that's *delizioso*!

4 boneless, skinless chicken breast halves (1 to 1½ pounds total), pounded to ¼-inch thickness
¼ teaspoon salt
¼ teaspoon black pepper
½ cup all-purpose flour

2 eggs, lightly beaten
¼ cup (½ stick) butter
⅓ cup Soave or other dry white wine
1 tablespoon capers
1 lemon, cut in half

Season the chicken with the salt and pepper. Place the flour in a shallow dish. Place the beaten eggs in another shallow dish. Coat the chicken breasts with the flour, then dip in the eggs. Meanwhile, melt the butter in a large skillet over medium-high heat. Cook the chicken for 3 to 4 minutes per side, until golden. Add the wine and capers to the skillet and squeeze the lemon over the chicken. Cook for 2 to 4 more minutes, or until the chicken is cooked through and the sauce begins to glaze the chicken breasts.

NOTE: To make Veal with Capers, just substitute about 1 pound of pounded veal cutlets for the chicken breasts, cooking in more than one batch if necessary.

Stuffed Chicken Muffins

6 servings

There's more than muffins baking in *this* muffin tin. Here's the secret to making those restaurant-style stuffed chicken breasts . . . Italian-style!

½ cup ricotta cheese
¼ cup grated Parmesan cheese
1 can (2¼ ounces) sliced black
   olives, drained
1 teaspoon dried oregano
1 teaspoon garlic powder
½ teaspoon salt

½ teaspoon black pepper
6 boneless, skinless chicken
   breast halves (1½ to 2
   pounds total), pounded to
   ¼-inch thickness
1 teaspoon olive oil
⅛ teaspoon paprika

Preheat the oven to 350°F. In a medium-sized bowl, combine the ricotta and Parmesan cheeses, the olives, oregano, garlic powder, salt, and pepper; mix well. Spoon the mixture evenly onto the center of the chicken breasts. Roll each chicken breast tightly,

tucking in the sides as you roll. Place each roll seam side down in its own cup of a regular muffin tin that has been coated with nonstick cooking spray. In a small bowl, combine the oil and paprika, then brush it over the tops of the chicken. Place the muffin tin on a cookie sheet and bake for 25 to 30 minutes, or until no pink remains and the juices run clear.

NOTE: Place the chicken under the broiler for the last 5 minutes of cooking to brown the tops; or top with your favorite spaghetti sauce.

All-in-One Chicken

4 to 6 servings

If you think one-dish meals tend to be dull and bland, you haven't tasted this one! Talk about zip . . . !

1 pound hot Italian sausage, cut into 1-inch pieces
1½ pounds boneless, skinless chicken breasts, cut into 1-inch chunks
½ of a large sweet onion, thickly sliced
5 garlic cloves, coarsely chopped
½ teaspoon salt
½ teaspoon black pepper
¼ pound fresh mushrooms, sliced
1 jar (7 ounces) roasted red peppers, drained and chopped
8 peperoncini
1 can (15 ounces) sliced white potatoes, drained
¼ cup chopped fresh parsley

In a large skillet, brown the sausage over medium heat for 10 minutes. Add the chicken, onion, garlic, salt, and pepper and cook for 5 minutes, or until no pink remains in the chicken. Add the mushrooms, roasted peppers, peperoncini, potatoes, and parsley and stir until well combined. Reduce the heat to low, cover, and simmer for 5 to 7 minutes, or until the mushrooms are tender and the potatoes are heated through.

NOTE: If you want to cut back on the spiciness of this dish, use a mild sausage and omit the peperoncini.

Lemony Garlic Chicken

3 to 4 servings

The subtle blend of flavors in this marinade always has my guests trying to guess the ingredients. It sure makes dinner fun!

⅔ cup lemon juice (juice of 4 to 5 lemons)
⅓ cup dry white wine
3 tablespoons olive oil
¼ cup chopped fresh parsley
1 garlic bulb, cloves separated, peeled, and chopped

One 3- to 3½-pound chicken, cut into 8 pieces
½ teaspoon salt
½ teaspoon black pepper

In a large bowl, combine the lemon juice, wine, oil, parsley, and garlic. Sprinkle the chicken with the salt and pepper and place in a 9″ × 13″ baking dish that has been coated with nonstick cooking spray. Pour the lemon mixture over the chicken, cover, and marinate for 20 to 30 minutes in the refrigerator. Preheat the oven to 375°F. Bake the chicken, uncovered, for 60 to 70 minutes, or until no pink remains and the juices run clear.

Jiffy Chicken Surprise

Has your gang got the boring-dinner blues? Here's a great tip for a treat you can make in a jiffy. Keep an extra package of chicken breasts in the freezer and wake things up with a mouth-watering surprise!

¾ cup ricotta cheese
1 can (4 ounces) mushroom stems and pieces, drained
2 tablespoons grated Parmesan cheese
1 tablespoon olive oil
¼ teaspoon salt, divided
¼ teaspoon black pepper, divided

6 boneless, skinless chicken breast halves (1½ to 2 pounds total), pounded to ¼-inch thickness
3 tablespoons Italian-flavored bread crumbs
Nonstick cooking spray

Preheat the oven to 350°F. In a small bowl, combine the ricotta cheese, mushrooms, Parmesan cheese, oil, ⅛ teaspoon salt, and ⅛ teaspoon pepper. Spread the mixture evenly over the tops of the chicken breasts and roll up jelly-roll style. Place seam side down in an 8-inch square baking dish that has been coated with nonstick cooking spray. Sprinkle with the remaining ⅛ teaspoon each salt and pepper, then with the bread crumbs. Coat the bread crumbs with nonstick cooking spray. Bake for 25 to 30 minutes, or until the chicken is golden and the juices run clear.

NOTE: Serve with warm spaghetti sauce for spooning over the top.

Fast Chicken in Pepper Sauce

6 servings

It's a cinch to cook like an Italian chef—just spice things up a bit. One taste of this festive dish, and it's like a tour of Italy without ever leaving home.

½ cup all-purpose flour
1 teaspoon salt, divided
¼ teaspoon white pepper
2 eggs, lightly beaten
4 tablespoons (½ stick) butter, divided
¼ cup olive oil, divided

6 boneless, skinless chicken breast halves (1½ to 2 pounds total), pounded to ¼-inch thickness
1 jar (12 ounces) roasted peppers, drained
1 cup (½ pint) heavy cream

In a shallow dish, combine the flour with ½ teaspoon salt and ⅛ teaspoon white pepper. Place the beaten eggs in another shallow dish. In a large skillet, melt 2 tablespoons butter with 2 tablespoons oil over medium-high heat. Coat the chicken breasts with the flour mixture and then dip in the eggs, coating completely. Cook half the chicken for 3 to 4 minutes per side, or until golden. Remove the chicken to a platter and cover to keep warm. Wipe out the skillet with a paper towel and heat the remaining 2 tablespoons butter and the remaining oil; cook the remaining 3 chicken breasts. Meanwhile, combine the roasted peppers, cream, and the remaining ½ teaspoon salt and ⅛ teaspoon white pepper in a blender or a food processor that has been fitted with its metal cutting blade and process for a few seconds, or until the peppers are chopped and the mixture is well combined. Pour into the skillet, then return the chicken to the skillet and cook for 4 to 5 minutes, or until heated through.

Crispy Parmesan Chicken

3 to 4 servings

When you can't dine out and don't have a lot of time to spend in the kitchen, this easy "Chicken Parm" can be the best of both worlds.

1 can (8 ounces) tomato sauce
1 envelope (1½ ounces) dry spaghetti sauce mix
1 cup dry bread crumbs

⅓ cup grated Parmesan cheese
One 3- to 3½-pound chicken, cut into 8 pieces
2 tablespoons vegetable oil

Preheat the oven to 400°F. Pour the tomato sauce into a shallow dish. In another shallow dish, combine the sauce mix, bread crumbs, and Parmesan cheese. Dip the chicken pieces into the tomato sauce, then into the bread crumb mixture, coating completely. Place the chicken in a 9" × 13" baking dish that has been coated with nonstick cooking spray and drizzle with the oil. Bake for 50 to 55 minutes, or until no pink remains and the juices run clear.

NOTE: For a complete dinner, serve this with spaghetti and marinara sauce, making sure to have some extra warm sauce for topping the chicken.

Prizewinning Lemon Chicken

6 servings

No contest here—chicken smothered in tart lemon sauce and dotted with capers gets first prize for its sunny flavor!

½ cup all-purpose flour
½ teaspoon salt
½ teaspoon black pepper
6 boneless, skinless chicken breast halves (1½ to 2 pounds total)
4 tablespoons (½ stick) butter, divided

2 tablespoons olive oil
1 can (14 ounces) artichoke hearts, drained and quartered
½ cup dry white wine
Juice of 1 lemon
1 tablespoon capers, rinsed and drained

In a shallow dish, combine the flour, salt, and pepper. Coat the chicken with the flour mixture and set aside. Heat 2 tablespoons butter and the oil in a large skillet over medium heat. Cook the chicken for 4 to 5 minutes per side, or until golden brown. Remove the chicken to a platter, then add the remaining 2 tablespoons butter to the skillet. Add the artichoke hearts, wine, lemon juice, and capers. Cook for 2 to 3 minutes, or until bubbly, stirring occasionally. Return the chicken to the skillet, cover, and reduce the heat to low. Cook for 12 to 15 minutes, or until the chicken is cooked through and the sauce has thickened slightly.

No-Toil Chicken in Foil

4 servings

Most everybody loves to eat, but I don't know anybody who loves scrubbing those hard-to-clean baking pans. The gang will be thrilled when you have this tasty winner, 'cause making it in foil means that the cleanup crew gets the night off!

1 envelope (0.7 ounce) dry Italian dressing mix
4 boneless, skinless chicken breast halves (1 to 1½ pounds total)
2 bell peppers (1 red and 1 green), cut into 1-inch chunks

1 zucchini, cut into ½-inch slices
1 medium-sized onion, cut in half and then into ½-inch slices
½ cup Italian dressing
1 cup (4 ounces) shredded mozzarella cheese

Preheat the oven to 450°F. Place the dry dressing mix in a shallow dish. Coat both sides of the chicken breasts evenly with the mix. Lay each piece of chicken on a piece of aluminum foil about 12″ × 18″. In a large bowl, combine the bell peppers, zucchini, onion, and Italian dressing; toss until the vegetables are well mixed and completely coated. Place evenly over the chicken breasts. Drizzle any remaining dressing over the vegetables. Place ¼ cup mozzarella cheese on top of each breast and seal the foil packages tightly. Place on a rimmed baking sheet and bake for 30 to 35 minutes, or until no pink remains in the chicken and the juices run clear. Serve the chicken in the foil, carefully opening the packages to allow the steam to escape.

NOTE: I like to let adult guests open their own chicken packets at the table, but if you do that, make sure they're very careful. The steam from inside the packets is very hot!

Five-Star Chicken

4 servings

Tasty enough to be found at the finest restaurants, and easy enough to make at home!

¼ cup all-purpose flour
½ teaspoon salt
½ teaspoon black pepper
4 boneless, skinless chicken
  breast halves (1 to 1½
  pounds total)
¼ cup (½ stick) butter
½ cup chicken broth

¼ cup dry red wine
½ pound fresh mushrooms,
  quartered
1 large tomato, chopped
1 small onion, chopped
2 tablespoons chopped fresh
  parsley

In a shallow dish, combine the flour, salt, and pepper and coat the chicken evenly on both sides. In a large skillet, melt the butter over medium-high heat and sauté the chicken for 4 to 5 minutes per side, or until browned. Remove the chicken to a platter and set aside. Add the remaining ingredients to the skillet and cook for about 5 minutes, stirring occasionally. Return the chicken to the skillet and reduce the heat to medium-low. Simmer for 5 to 7 minutes, or until the sauce thickens and the chicken is warmed through.

NOTE: If the chicken breasts are very thick, flatten them a bit by pounding with a kitchen mallet.

Tricolored Chicken Kebabs

4 to 6 servings

Triple the fun, these colorful kebabs will disappear quicker than you can say 1–2–3!

12 wooden or metal skewers
2 pounds boneless, skinless
 chicken breasts, cut into
 36 chunks
1 large green bell pepper, cut
 into 12 chunks

1 large red bell pepper, cut into
 12 chunks
1 bottle (8 ounces) Italian
 dressing

Preheat the broiler. If using wooden skewers, soak them in water for 15 to 20 minutes. In a large bowl, combine all the ingredients and toss to coat. Thread the chicken and pepper pieces alternately onto the skewers so that there are 3 pieces of chicken, 1 piece of red pepper, and 1 piece of green pepper on each one. Place the skewers on a large rimmed baking sheet that has been lined with aluminum foil and coated with nonstick cooking spray. Broil for 10 to 12 minutes, or until no pink remains in the chicken and the juices run clear, turning halfway through the broiling.

NOTE: We soak the wooden skewers in water beforehand so that they won't burn under the broiler.

Cornish Hens in Chianti Sauce

2 to 4 servings

Delicate little Cornish hens deserve the special treatment of wine and herbs. So do we!

2 Cornish hens
½ teaspoon salt, divided
½ teaspoon black pepper, divided
2 scallions
½ of a lemon, cut in half

½ cup Chianti or other dry red wine
2 tablespoons butter, melted
1 garlic clove, minced
½ teaspoon dried rosemary

Preheat the oven to 375°F. Season the cavities of the hens with ¼ teaspoon salt and ¼ teaspoon pepper. Fold the scallions in thirds and place 1 in the cavity of each hen along with a lemon quarter. Place the hens breast side up in an 8-inch square baking dish. In a small bowl, combine the Chianti, butter, garlic, and rosemary. Pour over the hens, then sprinkle with the remaining ¼ teaspoon salt and ¼ teaspoon pepper. Bake for 55 to 60 minutes, or until no pink remains and the juices run clear, basting frequently. Serve whole, or cut each hen in half.

NOTE: Make sure to serve these with plenty of the Chianti sauce from the pan.

Prosciutto-Provolone-Turkey Roll-ups

4 to 6 servings

Ham, cheese, and turkey . . . sounds like a sandwich to me. But no, it's not a sandwich, it's a main dish that's company-elegant and family-friendly at the same time.

8 turkey breast cutlets (1½ to 2 pounds total), pounded to ¼-inch thickness (see Note)
¼ pound prosciutto or ham, cut into 8 thin slices
8 slices (8 ounces) provolone cheese

¼ teaspoon black pepper
1 tablespoon grated Parmesan cheese
2 tablespoons Italian-flavored bread crumbs
Nonstick cooking spray

Preheat the oven to 375°F. Place the turkey cutlets on a work surface and top each with 1 slice of prosciutto and 1 slice of provolone cheese. Roll up jelly-roll style and place seam side down in an 8-inch square baking dish that has been coated with nonstick cooking spray. Sprinkle evenly with the pepper and then with the Parmesan cheese and bread crumbs. Coat the tops with nonstick cooking spray and bake for 20 to 25 minutes, or until the turkey is no longer pink and the bread crumbs are golden.

NOTE: If thin cutlets aren't available in the meat case of your supermarket, have the butcher cut a turkey breast into thin cutlets for you.

Turkey Cacciatore Meatballs

about 24 meatballs

Sauce on the inside, sauce on the outside . . . plus a load of flavor in each bite!

1 pound ground turkey
1 cup Italian-flavored bread
  crumbs
½ cup grated Parmesan cheese
½ of a medium-sized green
  bell pepper, finely chopped
½ of a medium-sized onion,
  finely chopped

1 jar (28 ounces) spaghetti
  sauce, divided
2 eggs
2 teaspoons garlic powder
1 teaspoon dried oregano
½ teaspoon salt
½ teaspoon black pepper
¼ cup olive oil

In a large bowl, combine the turkey, bread crumbs, Parmesan cheese, green pepper, onion, ¼ cup spaghetti sauce, the eggs, garlic powder, oregano, salt, and black pepper. With your hands, combine the mixture until thoroughly mixed. Form into about 24 meatballs; set aside. In a large pot, heat the oil over medium-high heat. Place the meatballs in the pot a few at a time and brown for 2 to 3 minutes, turning to brown on all sides. Drain off the excess liquid and add the remaining spaghetti sauce to the pot; reduce the heat to low, cover, and simmer for 18 to 20 minutes, or until the meatballs are cooked through.

Italian Turkey Burgers

6 servings

By itself, ground turkey tends to be a bit bland. But give it an Italian accent and it'll have more zest than any hamburger ever dreamed of!

1 pound ground turkey
1 pound bulk hot Italian turkey
   sausage
¼ cup Italian-flavored bread
   crumbs

¼ cup grated Parmesan cheese
¼ cup water
1 teaspoon garlic powder
1 teaspoon onion powder

In a large bowl, combine all the ingredients; mix well. Shape into 6 patties and set aside. Coat a large skillet with nonstick cooking spray. Add half the patties, cover, and cook over medium-high heat for 10 to 12 minutes, or until the turkey is no longer pink, turning halfway through the cooking; repeat with the remaining patties. Keep the first batch warm in a low oven until all are cooked.

NOTE: Serve on hamburger buns with lettuce, tomato slices, and your favorite condiments.

Meats
Carne

continued

Mom's Veal in Tomato-Mushroom Sauce

4 servings

This was a really popular dish at our house when I was a kid. The kitchen sure smelled great when Mom was making it, and we kids couldn't wait to dip crusty bread chunks into the hearty sauce she served it up with.

1 pound veal cutlets, pounded to ¼-inch thickness and cut into medallions
1 teaspoon salt
⅛ teaspoon black pepper
½ cup all-purpose flour
¼ cup (½ stick) butter or margarine
1 cup sweet Marsala wine

½ cup chicken or beef broth
Juice of ½ lemon
1 can (14 ounces) whole tomatoes, drained and coarsely chopped
¼ pound fresh mushrooms, sliced
½ teaspoon dried oregano

Season the veal with the salt and pepper. Place the flour in a shallow dish and coat the veal with the flour. In a large skillet, melt the butter over medium heat. Add the veal and brown for about 1 minute per side; if necessary, brown the veal in batches. Drain on paper towels. Return the browned veal to the skillet (if necessary) and add the remaining ingredients. Simmer for 8 to 10 minutes, until the veal is cooked through and the sauce is thickened, stirring occasionally. Serve immediately.

NOTE: Since this veal is so saucy, I like to serve it over hot cooked pasta.

Veal with Vodka Sauce

4 to 5 servings

Don't worry about your guests getting tipsy, 'cause the alcohol you put in here gets cooked off, even though the distinctive vodka flavor remains.

½ cup all-purpose flour
2 teaspoons salt, divided
1 to 1¼ pounds veal cutlets,
   pounded to ¼-inch
   thickness
¼ cup (½ stick) butter, divided

2 tablespoons olive oil
1 small onion, finely chopped
1 cup canned crushed tomatoes
½ cup heavy cream
1 teaspoon black pepper
⅓ cup vodka

In a shallow dish, combine the flour and 1 teaspoon salt; mix well. Completely coat the veal with the flour mixture. In a large skillet, melt 2 tablespoons butter over medium-high heat; sauté the cutlets for about 2 minutes per side, or until slightly browned; if necessary, sauté the veal in batches. Remove the cooked veal to a covered platter to keep warm. Heat the remaining 2 tablespoons butter and the oil in the skillet over medium heat. Add the onion and sauté for 2 minutes, just until tender. Add the tomatoes, cream, pepper, and the remaining 1 teaspoon salt. Cook for 1 minute, stirring occasionally. Add the vodka and simmer for 2 minutes, or until the sauce thickens, stirring occasionally. Add the veal and continue simmering for 3 to 4 minutes, or until the veal is heated through. Serve immediately.

Veal Marsala

4 servings

Italians perfected the preparation of veal, and this is one of their perfect veal dishes. I guess that's why it's considered a classic.

¼ cup all-purpose flour
1 teaspoon salt
½ teaspoon black pepper
1 pound veal cutlets, pounded
   to ¼-inch thickness
2 tablespoons olive oil
2 garlic cloves, minced

½ pound fresh mushrooms,
   sliced
2 tablespoons butter
2 tablespoons chopped fresh
   parsley
1 cup sweet Marsala wine

In a shallow dish, combine the flour, salt, and pepper. Coat the veal with the flour mixture. In a large skillet, heat the oil over medium-high heat. Sauté the garlic and veal for 4 to 5 minutes, until the veal is browned, turning halfway through the cooking. Remove the veal to a platter; set aside. Add the mushrooms, butter, and parsley to the skillet and cook until the mushrooms are tender, stirring occasionally. Stir in the wine, then return the veal to the skillet and cook for 3 to 5 minutes, until the sauce thickens and the veal is warmed through, turning halfway through the cooking. Serve immediately.

NOTE: No fresh mushrooms? It's okay to use canned or even to leave them out completely.

Osso Buco

4 servings

Osso Buco is one of my all-time favorite dishes. Why? Because it's succulent veal shanks in a mouthwateringly flavorful sauce! Now, tell me, can *you* resist it?

¼ cup all-purpose flour
¼ teaspoon black pepper
4 veal shanks (12 to 14 ounces each)
3 tablespoons vegetable oil
1 can (10¾ ounces) condensed onion soup
1 cup dry white wine
½ cup plus 2 tablespoons water, divided
2 tablespoons lemon juice

1 medium-sized tomato, chopped
1 tablespoon chopped fresh parsley
½ teaspoon garlic powder
3 tablespoons cornstarch
2 cans (14½ ounces each) whole potatoes, drained
1 can (14½ ounces) diced carrots, drained

In a shallow dish, combine the flour and pepper. Coat the shanks with the flour mixture. In a large pot, heat the oil over medium-high heat and brown the shanks, about 5 minutes per side. Add the soup, wine, ½ cup water, the lemon juice, tomato, parsley, and garlic powder; reduce the heat to low, cover, and simmer for 2 hours, or until the veal is tender, stirring occasionally. In a small bowl, combine the cornstarch and the remaining 2 tablespoons water until smooth; stir into the pot and mix until the sauce thickens. Add the potatoes and carrots and simmer for 10 to 15 minutes, until heated through.

Asiago Veal Rolls

6 servings

You might have to search a bit to find Asiago cheese, but it's so special, it's well worth looking for.

6 veal cutlets (about 1 pound total), pounded to ¼-inch thickness
½ teaspoon dried basil
½ teaspoon salt
¼ teaspoon black pepper
¼ pound Asiago cheese, cut into 6 chunks (see Note on page xxi)
2 tablespoons olive oil
1 can (14½ ounces) diced tomatoes, undrained
1 can (14 ounces) artichoke hearts, drained and quartered
1 teaspoon garlic powder

Sprinkle the veal cutlets on both sides with the basil, salt, and pepper. Place a piece of cheese in the center of each cutlet and roll up; secure each with a toothpick. Heat the oil in a large skillet over medium-high heat until hot but not smoking. Place the veal rolls in the skillet and brown for about 4 minutes, turning to brown on all sides. Add the remaining ingredients and bring to a simmer; cook for 5 more minutes, or until the veal is cooked through and the cheese is melted. **Remove the toothpicks before serving.**

Veal Chops with Sun-dried Tomatoes

4 servings

Sun-dried tomatoes are showing up in all sorts of great recipes, and the first time I tasted them in this, I knew it was a dish that was going to be showing up on my table again and again!

⅓ cup all-purpose flour
4 veal rib chops (about 2 pounds total), 1 inch thick
2 tablespoons olive oil
1 can (14 ounces) artichoke hearts, drained and quartered
¼ cup sun-dried tomatoes in oil, drained and cut in half

¼ cup coarsely chopped fresh basil
⅓ cup dry white wine
¼ cup water
¼ teaspoon salt
¼ teaspoon black pepper

Place the flour in a shallow dish and coat the chops evenly with it. In a large skillet, heat the oil over medium-high heat and brown the chops for 4 to 5 minutes per side. Remove the chops to a platter and add the remaining ingredients to the skillet; mix well. Return the chops to the skillet and reduce the heat to low. Cook for 5 to 6 more minutes, or to desired doneness.

NOTE: For even more sun-dried tomato flavor, brown the chops in the oil from the tomatoes instead of in olive oil.

Garden Eggplant Meat Loaf

6 to 8 servings

Want to serve something that everyone likes, is easy to fix, and makes you look like a real kitchen pro? Garden meat loaf is it! And this one tastes great the first time around, as well as making "vealy" good leftover cold meat loaf sandwiches. . . . I promise!

½ of a medium-sized eggplant, peeled and cut into 1-inch cubes
1 medium-sized onion, quartered
2 garlic cloves
¼ cup olive oil

2 pounds ground veal
3 eggs
1 cup Italian-flavored bread crumbs
¼ cup grated Parmesan cheese
1 tablespoon Italian seasoning
1 teaspoon black pepper

Preheat the oven to 350°F. Place the eggplant, onion, garlic, and oil in a food processor that has been fitted with its metal cutting blade. Process for 15 to 20 seconds, or until the vegetables are finely chopped. Place the mixture in a medium-sized skillet and cook over medium heat for 8 to 10 minutes, stirring, until well cooked. Remove from the heat. In a large bowl, combine the remaining ingredients; mix well. Add the vegetable mixture to the meat mixture; mix well. On a rimmed baking sheet that has been coated with nonstick cooking spray, form the mixture into a 5" × 12" loaf. Bake for 1¼ to 1½ hours, or until the juices run clear. Allow to sit for 5 minutes before slicing.

Tied-up Breast of Veal

6 to 8 servings

Making this doesn't tie you up for long, but it sure will look and taste like you're a kitchen hero!

1 teaspoon onion powder
1 teaspoon garlic powder
1 teaspoon Italian seasoning
1 teaspoon salt
⅛ teaspoon black pepper
1 tablespoon olive oil
One 3- to 4-pound boneless breast of veal, rolled and tied (see Note)

1 can (14½ ounces) ready-to-use chicken broth
¾ cup water, divided
2 tablespoons all-purpose flour

Preheat the oven to 450°F. In a small bowl, combine the onion powder, garlic powder, Italian seasoning, salt, pepper, and olive oil; mix well. Rub the mixture over the veal, coating evenly. Pour

the chicken broth into an ungreased 9" × 13" baking dish and place the veal in the dish. Bake for 30 minutes, then reduce the heat to 350°F. and roast for an additional 50 to 60 minutes, until a meat thermometer reaches 160°F., or until desired doneness, basting occasionally. Remove the veal from the pan and add ¼ cup water to the drippings, stirring to loosen all the drippings. Transfer the liquid to a medium-sized saucepan and bring to a boil over medium-high heat. Meanwhile, in a small bowl, whisk the remaining ½ cup water with the flour until smooth. Slowly add to the drippings, stirring constantly until the gravy is thickened. Remove from the heat and serve over the sliced veal.

NOTE: Your butcher should be happy to roll and tie a boneless veal breast for you—just ask.

Braciola

Italians are masters at turning inexpensive cuts of meat into masterpieces. This one is no exception.

1 cup Italian-flavored bread
   crumbs
¼ cup grated Romano cheese
¼ pound Genoa or other
   salami, finely chopped
2 eggs
½ teaspoon black pepper

1½ pounds beef rump roast,
   cut into ⅛-inch slices
   (see Note)
¼ cup olive oil
1 jar (28 ounces) spaghetti
   sauce

In a small bowl, combine the bread crumbs, cheese, salami, eggs, and pepper; mix well. Spread the mixture evenly over the slices of beef; roll up jelly-roll style and secure each with a toothpick. In a large pot, heat the oil over medium-high heat and brown the beef rolls for 6 minutes, turning to brown on all sides. Reduce the heat to low and add the spaghetti sauce; cover and simmer for 35 to 40 minutes, or until the beef is tender. **Remove the toothpicks before serving.**

NOTE: Just ask the butcher to cut the rump roast into thin slices for you—it's easier and safer than doing it yourself.

Italian Beef Stew

4 to 6 servings

If there's anything homier and more heart-warming than beef stew, I don't know what it is . . . unless it's *Italian* beef stew.

2 tablespoons olive oil
2½ pounds boneless beef chuck roast, trimmed and cut into 1-inch chunks
1 large onion, coarsely chopped
2 cans (14½ ounces each) Italian-style stewed tomatoes, undrained
1 can (14½ ounces) ready-to-use beef broth

1 can (4 ounces) mushroom stems and pieces, undrained
3 large red potatoes, cut into large chunks
3 large carrots, cut into large chunks
½ teaspoon salt
¼ teaspoon black pepper

In a large pot, heat the oil over medium-high heat. Add the beef and onion and cook for 8 to 10 minutes, or until the beef is browned, stirring frequently. Add the remaining ingredients and bring to a boil. Reduce the heat to medium-low, cover, and simmer for 60 to 70 minutes, or until the meat is tender.

NOTE: Serve this over warm buttered noodles or rice to enjoy every last drop of the sauce.

Italian Cubed Steak

4 servings

When you need a way to turn inexpensive cubed steak into a company-worthy entrée, this is it.

¼ cup all-purpose flour
½ teaspoon paprika
¼ teaspoon black pepper
Four 6-ounce beef cubed steaks
1 can (14½ ounces) Italian-
   style stewed tomatoes,
   undrained

1 cup condensed beef broth
1 teaspoon garlic powder
¼ cup water
2 tablespoons cornstarch

In a shallow dish, combine the flour, paprika, and pepper; add the steaks and turn to coat lightly. Coat a large skillet with non-stick cooking spray and heat over medium-high heat. Cook the steaks for 10 to 14 minutes, or until no pink remains, turning halfway through the cooking. Remove the steaks to a platter and cover to keep warm. Reduce the heat to medium and add the stewed tomatoes, broth, and garlic powder to the skillet. Heat, stirring occasionally, just until the mixture begins to boil. In a small bowl, combine the water and cornstarch; stir until smooth. Slowly add to the tomato mixture and stir until thickened and smooth. Return the steaks to the pan and cook until thoroughly heated. Serve immediately.

NOTE: These also make great sandwiches. Just place each steak on a split hoagie roll and top with the sauce.

Simmering Chuck Roast

6 to 8 servings

So juicy, so tender . . . without even turning on the oven!

2 tablespoons olive oil
One 4- to 5-pound boneless
   beef chuck roast
1 tablespoon onion powder
1 tablespoon garlic powder
1 tablespoon dried oregano

2 teaspoons salt
¼ teaspoon black pepper
5 large onions, chopped
1 can (28 ounces) diced
   tomatoes, undrained

In a large pot, heat the oil over medium-high heat and brown the roast for 8 minutes, turning to brown on all sides. Sprinkle the onion powder, garlic powder, oregano, salt, and pepper over the roast, then add the onions and tomatoes to the pot. Reduce the heat to low, cover, and simmer for about 3 hours, or until the roast is tender. Slice the roast and serve with the pan juices.

Braised Mediterranean Beef

4 to 6 servings

Sounds fancy, doesn't it? The bottom line is that this one-pot recipe makes short work of an elegant-tasting dish!

⅓ cup vegetable oil
3 pounds boneless beef chuck
   roast, cut into 1-inch cubes
2 large onions, chopped
4 celery stalks, diced
4 garlic cloves, minced
2 cans (28 ounces each)
   Italian-style stewed
   tomatoes, chopped, juice
   reserved

1 cup dry white wine
1 cup chopped fresh parsley
1 teaspoon dried oregano
1½ teaspoons salt
1 teaspoon black pepper

In a large pot, heat the oil over medium-high heat and brown the beef on all sides. Add the onions, celery, and garlic and sauté until the vegetables are tender. Add the remaining ingredients (including the juice from the tomatoes) and bring to a boil. Reduce the heat to low, cover, and simmer for 1½ to 2 hours, or until the beef is fork-tender.

NOTE: For rosemary-flavored beef, substitute dried rosemary for the oregano.

Steak Pizzaiola

2 to 4 servings

When I want to make a really good impression, I serve up this simple yet classic Italian recipe.

2 boneless beef strip steaks (8 to 10 ounces each), 1 inch thick
¼ teaspoon onion powder
¼ teaspoon garlic powder
¼ teaspoon salt
¼ teaspoon black pepper
2 tablespoons olive oil

1 medium-sized onion, thinly sliced
1 green bell pepper, cut into thin strips
1 can (14½ ounces) Italian-style diced tomatoes, undrained

Season the steaks on both sides with the onion powder, garlic powder, salt, and black pepper. In a large skillet, heat the oil over medium-high heat. Brown the steaks for 2 minutes per side. Reduce the heat to medium and add the onion, green pepper, and diced tomatoes, then cover and cook for 5 minutes. Uncover and cook for 7 to 10 more minutes, or to desired doneness, turning the steaks halfway through the cooking.

NOTE: For great steak sandwiches, thinly slice the steaks and serve on sandwich rolls with the vegetables and sauce.

My Own Italian Meatballs

12 meatballs

Everyone has a favorite meatball recipe and, believe me, I've tried tons of 'em! In *my* book, this one takes first place.

1 pound ground beef
¾ cup plain dry bread crumbs
½ cup grated Parmesan cheese
½ cup water
¼ cup coarsely chopped fresh
   parsley

1 egg
1½ teaspoons garlic powder
1 teaspoon salt
1 teaspoon black pepper

Preheat the oven to 350°F. In a large bowl, combine all the ingredients; mix well. Form the mixture into 12 meatballs and place on a rimmed baking sheet that has been coated with nonstick cooking spray. Bake for 25 to 30 minutes, or until no pink remains.

NOTE: You can also brown the meatballs in a large pot over medium-high heat and then complete the cooking by simmering in your favorite sauce. And for a complete meal, serve over hot cooked pasta.

Rice Balls

12 rice balls

If you like arranging food into various shapes for fancier serving, you're gonna have a load of fun with this "ball game"!

¾ pound lean ground beef
¾ cup spaghetti sauce
¾ cup ricotta cheese
¾ cup (3 ounces) shredded
   mozzarella cheese
1 tablespoon garlic powder
1 teaspoon Italian seasoning

¼ teaspoon salt
¼ teaspoon black pepper
6 cups cooked white rice
½ cup grated Parmesan cheese
¼ cup plain dry bread crumbs
Nonstick cooking spray

Preheat the oven to 375°F. Brown the beef in a large skillet over medium-high heat, stirring to break up the meat as it cooks; drain off any excess liquid. Remove from the heat and stir in the spaghetti sauce, the ricotta and mozzarella cheeses, the garlic powder, Italian seasoning, salt, and pepper; mix well. Meanwhile, in a medium-sized bowl, combine the cooked rice and the Parmesan cheese; mix well. Spray a 12-cup muffin tin with nonstick cooking spray. Place 1 heaping tablespoon of the rice mixture in each cup. Using the back of a spoon, make an indentation in each mound of rice, and fill evenly with the meat mixture. Cover evenly with the remaining rice, forming a mound on top. Sprinkle with the bread crumbs and coat with vegetable spray. Bake for 25 to 30 minutes, or until heated through and the tops are golden. Using a large spoon, remove each rice ball from the muffin tin and serve.

Sicilian Meatball Sandwiches

4 sandwiches

Nothing's more satisfying than a thick hot sandwich bursting with fill-ya-up satisfaction—and this one's got it all!

1 jar (28 ounces) spaghetti sauce, divided
½ cup fresh bread crumbs
1 small onion, finely chopped
¼ cup grated Parmesan or Romano cheese
1 egg
1 teaspoon dried parsley flakes
1 teaspoon garlic powder
1 pound ground beef
Four 6-inch Italian sandwich rolls

Preheat the oven to 350°F. In a large bowl, combine ⅓ cup of the spaghetti sauce, the bread crumbs, onion, cheese, egg, parsley flakes, and garlic powder; mix well. Add the ground beef and blend well. Shape into sixteen 2-inch meatballs and arrange in a 9″ × 13″ baking pan. Bake for 20 minutes. Remove from the oven and drain off the liquid. Pour the remaining sauce over the meatballs and return to the oven for 10 to 15 minutes, or until hot and completely cooked. Serve the meatballs and sauce on the sandwich rolls.

NOTE: I like to sprinkle the meatballs with some additional Parmesan cheese just before serving.

Rosemary-Roasted Rack of Lamb

4 to 6 servings

Think this is too fancy-schmancy to prepare? Not at all! You and your guests are in for a treat, 'cause in less than an hour you can be sitting down to a feast fit for a king!

Two 1½-pound racks of lamb
1 tablespoon olive oil
1 teaspoon dried rosemary
2 teaspoons chopped fresh
  parsley

½ teaspoon paprika
1 teaspoon salt

Preheat the oven to 325°F. Brush both racks of lamb evenly with the oil. In a small bowl, combine the rosemary, parsley, paprika, and salt; sprinkle the seasoning mixture evenly over the lamb. Place the lamb in a roasting pan that has been coated with non-stick cooking spray. Bake for 50 to 55 minutes for medium-rare, or to desired doneness beyond that. Slice the racks into individual chops and serve immediately.

NOTE: You can also roast this as a crown roast of lamb by tying the two racks of lamb together to form a crown. (The easy way is to ask your butcher to do it for you!)

Pork Tenderloin alla Chianti

6 to 8 servings

Anytime you're feeling especially tender toward friends and family, this dish says it all . . . without a word from you.

1 can (10½ ounces) condensed beef broth
½ cup Chianti or other dry red wine
½ cup (1 stick) butter, melted
2 tablespoons olive oil, divided
2 garlic cloves, minced
1 teaspoon sugar
½ teaspoon dried oregano
2 pork tenderloins (about 1½ pounds total)
⅛ teaspoon salt
⅛ teaspoon black pepper
¼ cup water
2 tablespoons all-purpose flour

In a medium-sized bowl, combine the broth, wine, butter, 1 tablespoon oil, the garlic, sugar, and oregano; mix well. Rub the tenderloins with the remaining 1 tablespoon olive oil, the salt, and pepper. In a large skillet, brown the tenderloins over medium-high heat for 8 minutes, turning to brown on all sides. Add the broth mixture and bring to a boil. Reduce the heat to medium and cook for 10 to 12 minutes, or until the tenderloins are cooked through. In a small bowl, combine the water and flour, stirring until smooth. Add to the skillet and stir until well blended and the sauce has thickened. Cut the pork into ½-inch-thick slices and serve topped with the sauce.

Countryside Pork Chops

4 servings

You can take the pork chop out of the country, but you can't take the country out of this fresh-tasting dish.

¼ cup olive oil
2 yellow squash, cut into
   1-inch chunks
1 zucchini, cut into 1-inch
   chunks
1 medium-sized onion, cut into
   ¼-inch slices
4 pork loin chops (about 1½
   pounds total), 1 inch thick

¼ teaspoon salt
¼ teaspoon black pepper
½ pound fresh mushrooms,
   quartered
1 jar (28 ounces) spaghetti
   sauce
1 teaspoon dried oregano

In a large skillet, heat the oil over medium-high heat and sauté the yellow squash, zucchini, and onion for 4 to 6 minutes, or until tender. Transfer to a bowl and set aside. Season the pork chops with the salt and pepper and brown for 2 minutes per side. Return the sautéed vegetables to the skillet, reduce the heat to low, and add the mushrooms, spaghetti sauce, and oregano; cover and cook for 30 to 35 minutes, or until the pork chops are cooked through.

Lemon Pork Tenderloin

6 to 8 servings

This one's in the bag . . . really—'cause the juices and seasonings mix together to form one super sauce!

¼ cup plus 1 tablespoon olive oil, divided
Juice of 2 lemons (see Note)
1 jar (3¼ ounces) capers, undrained

4 garlic cloves, halved
2 pork tenderloins (about 1½ pounds total)
1 tablespoon sugar
½ teaspoon salt

In a large resealable plastic storage bag or a shallow dish, combine ¼ cup oil, the lemon juice, capers, and garlic; add the tenderloins. Seal the bag or cover the dish and refrigerate for 30 minutes, turning the tenderloins after 15 minutes. Heat the remaining 1 tablespoon oil in a large skillet over medium-high heat. Place the tenderloins in the skillet, reserving the marinade. Cook for 10 to 12 minutes, until cooked to medium, or to desired doneness beyond that, turning to brown on all sides. Remove to a cutting board and cover to keep warm. Place the reserved marinade, the sugar, and salt in the skillet and bring to a boil. Reduce the heat to low and simmer for 5 minutes. Slice the pork and serve topped with the sauce.

NOTE: The juice of 2 lemons is about ¼ cup. And sure, bottled lemon juice can be used if you don't have fresh lemons on hand.

Baked Pork Chops

4 servings

Thick and juicy, these oven-baked chops sure aim to please!

¼ cup olive oil
3 medium-sized onions, cut in
  half and sliced
5 bay leaves
4 center-cut pork loin chops
  (about 1½ pounds total),
  ¾ inch thick

1 egg, beaten
1 cup Italian-flavored bread
  crumbs
¼ teaspoon salt
¼ teaspoon black pepper
Nonstick cooking spray

Preheat the oven to 400°F. In a 9″ × 13″ baking dish, combine the oil, onions, and bay leaves. Place the egg in a shallow dish. Place the bread crumbs in another shallow dish. Dip the pork chops in the egg and then in the bread crumbs, coating completely. Place the chops on top of the onions and sprinkle with the salt and pepper; coat lightly with cooking spray. Bake for 35 to 40 minutes, or until the chops are cooked through. **Remove and discard the bay leaves before serving.**

Seafood
Frutti di Mare

Shrimp Scampi

4 to 6 servings

Without a doubt, this is shrimp at its best. Why? 'Cause it's bathed in butter, garlic, lemon, and parsley, that's why!

1 pound linguine
1 cup (2 sticks) butter
3 tablespoons olive oil
10 garlic cloves, minced
  (see Note)
1 teaspoon salt
½ teaspoon black pepper

1½ pounds large shrimp,
  peeled and deveined, tails
  left on
Juice of 1 lemon
2 tablespoons chopped fresh
  parsley

Cook the linguine according to the package directions and drain; keep warm. Meanwhile, in a large skillet, heat the butter and oil over medium heat. Add the garlic, salt, and pepper and sauté the garlic for 1 to 2 minutes; do not brown. Stir in the shrimp and cook for 3 to 4 minutes, just until pink. Stir in the lemon juice and parsley; mix well. Serve immediately over the warm linguine.

NOTE: I know 10 cloves of garlic sounds like a lot, but believe me, you can't have too much garlic in scampi!

Baked Flounder with Tomatoes

3 to 4 servings

When it's almost dinnertime and you're "flounder-ing" for something easy, here it is!

4 medium-sized plum
   tomatoes, chopped
1 teaspoon salt, divided
¼ teaspoon black pepper
1 pound flounder fillets

½ teaspoon dried oregano
1 tablespoon olive oil
1 tablespoon Italian-flavored
   bread crumbs

Preheat the oven to 350°F. Place the tomatoes in a 7″ × 11″ baking dish that has been coated with nonstick cooking spray. Sprinkle with ½ teaspoon salt and the pepper and lay the flounder over the top. Sprinkle with the remaining ½ teaspoon salt, the oregano, oil, and bread crumbs. Bake for 12 to 15 minutes, or until the fish flakes easily with a fork.

NOTE: The best thing about this recipe is that it's very light, so it works well with almost any type of white-fleshed fish.

Scallops Oreganata

We've tried this topping on clams, so now it's time to try it on scallops for that same taste of summer at the seashore.

¼ cup (½ stick) plus 1 tablespoon butter, melted
¼ cup Italian-flavored bread crumbs
2 tablespoons chopped fresh parsley

1 teaspoon dried oregano
1 teaspoon minced garlic
1 pound sea scallops
¼ teaspoon black pepper

Preheat the broiler. Coat an 8-inch square baking pan with 1 tablespoon butter and set aside. In a small bowl, combine the remaining ¼ cup butter, the bread crumbs, parsley, oregano, and garlic; mix well. Sprinkle the scallops with the pepper and place in the baking pan. Spoon the bread crumb mixture evenly over the scallops and broil for 8 to 10 minutes, or until the topping is golden and the scallops are cooked through.

NOTE: Watch the broiler carefully, because the scallops can go from golden to brown to burned very quickly.

Salmon with Wilted Spinach

4 servings

Hooray! A low-fat way to prepare our salmon *and* our veggies! Who could ask for anything more?

2 tablespoons olive oil
4 garlic cloves, minced
1 teaspoon salt, divided
¼ teaspoon black pepper
1 package (10 ounces) fresh
   spinach, washed and
   trimmed

4 salmon fillets (about
   1½ pounds total)
Juice of ½ lemon
¼ teaspoon dried basil

In a large pot, heat the oil over medium heat and add the garlic; sprinkle with ½ teaspoon salt and the pepper and sauté for 1 minute. Add the spinach and toss to coat. Place the salmon fillets over the spinach and sprinkle with the lemon juice, basil, and the remaining ½ teaspoon salt. Reduce the heat to medium-low, cover, and cook for 10 to 12 minutes, or until the spinach is wilted and the salmon flakes easily with a fork.

Tuna in Tomato-Anchovy Sauce

4 servings

Tuna is one of the meatiest types of fish, and this is really a super way to prepare it to make the most of its tempting taste and texture.

¼ cup all-purpose flour
1 teaspoon onion powder
1 teaspoon garlic powder
4 tuna steaks (about 1½ pounds total), 1 inch thick
1 tablespoon olive oil

½ cup water
½ cup dry white wine
1 tablespoon tomato paste
1 teaspoon anchovy paste
¼ teaspoon black pepper

In a shallow dish, combine the flour, onion powder, and garlic powder. Coat the tuna on all sides with the flour mixture. In a large skillet, heat the oil over medium-high heat and cook the fish for 2 to 3 minutes per side, or until golden. Remove the fish to a platter and cover to keep warm. Add the water, wine, tomato paste, anchovy paste, and pepper to the skillet; stir until smooth. Return the tuna to the skillet and cook for 4 to 5 minutes, or until the tuna is cooked to desired doneness. Place the tuna on the platter, spoon the sauce over it, and serve.

Amaretto Shrimp

4 to 5 servings

Even reading this recipe makes my mouth water. It just couldn't be any more delectable.

½ cup (1 stick) butter
⅓ cup amaretto (almond-flavored liqueur)
⅓ cup chopped blanched almonds

2 teaspoons sugar
½ teaspoon ground cinnamon
⅛ teaspoon cayenne pepper
1 pound large shrimp, peeled and deveined, tails left on

In a large skillet, melt the butter over medium heat. Add the amaretto, almonds, sugar, cinnamon, and cayenne pepper and stir until the sugar dissolves. Add the shrimp and cook for 3 to 5 minutes, just until pink. Serve immediately.

NOTE: I like to serve this over hot cooked rice so that I can savor every last bit of the amaretto sauce. Mmm, mmm!

Gustoso!

Short and Simple Pesto Fish

4 servings

This should get your attention: *only three ingredients!* And it's what I call a restaurant-fancy meal without the hefty price tag. Hooray!

2 cans (15 ounces each) sliced potatoes, drained
1 container (7 ounces) prepared pesto

4 flounder fillets (about 1½ pounds total)

Preheat the oven to 350°F. In a medium-sized bowl, combine the potatoes and half of the pesto sauce; toss until evenly coated. Place the mixture in a 9" × 13" baking dish that has been coated with nonstick cooking spray. Place the flounder over the potatoes and spread the remaining pesto sauce evenly over the fish, covering completely. Bake for 15 to 20 minutes, or until the fish flakes easily with a fork. Serve immediately.

NOTE: Since flounder fillets vary in thickness, you may get more than 4 fillets when buying 1½ pounds. Make sure to adjust the cooking time according to the thickness of the fish. Watch it carefully and allow the fish to cook until it flakes easily with a fork.

Not-Stuffed "Stuffed" Shrimp

4 to 5 servings

Why not eliminate the fuss and bother of stuffing shrimp? Here's how to take the easy way out and get the same great taste!

½ cup pimiento-stuffed green
  olives, chopped
½ cup (2 ounces) shredded
  Italian cheese blend
¼ cup Italian-flavored bread
  crumbs

1 tablespoon olive oil
1 pound large shrimp, peeled
  and deveined, tails left on
  (see Note)

Preheat the oven to 350°F. In a small bowl, combine all the ingredients except the shrimp until well mixed and crumbly. Place the shrimp in a single layer in a 9″ × 13″ baking dish that has been coated with nonstick cooking spray. Sprinkle the olive mixture evenly over the shrimp and bake for 13 to 15 minutes, or until the shrimp are cooked through.

NOTE: I like to leave the tails on the shrimp because they look better that way, but if you'd rather take them off, go ahead. It's easier to eat without them!

Zuppa de Clams

2 to 4 servings

No, it's not really soup, but this spiced-up clam broth would be a treat even without the succulent clams.

2 tablespoons olive oil
2 tablespoons chopped garlic
1 teaspoon crushed red pepper
1 can (28 ounces) Italian-style
    whole tomatoes, undrained

½ teaspoon sugar
½ teaspoon salt
2 dozen cherrystone or
    littleneck clams, cleaned
¼ cup chopped fresh parsley

In a large pot, heat the oil over medium-low heat. Add the garlic and red pepper and sauté for 2 to 3 minutes, or until the garlic is golden. Add the tomatoes, sugar, and salt; cover and simmer for 10 minutes. Add the clams, cover, and cook for 8 to 10 minutes, or until the clams open. **Discard any clams that do not open.** Stir in the parsley and serve.

NOTE: To make this a complete meal, serve the clams and sauce in bowls with lots of bread for dunking.

Parmesan Baked Fish

3 to 4 servings

Running late? Skip the fast food and cook something fast. This catch of the day will bake up melt-in-your-mouth delicious in no time!

⅓ cup all-purpose flour
½ teaspoon dried dillweed
¼ teaspoon onion powder
⅛ teaspoon salt
⅛ teaspoon black pepper
1 pound fresh or frozen white-fleshed fish fillets, such as cod, haddock, or whiting, thawed if frozen

2 tablespoons butter, melted
2 tablespoons grated Parmesan cheese

Preheat the oven to 450°F. In a shallow bowl, combine the flour, dillweed, onion powder, salt, and pepper; coat the fish fillets completely with the mixture. Place the fish in a 9″ × 13″ baking dish that has been coated with nonstick cooking spray. Drizzle the melted butter over the fish, then sprinkle with the Parmesan cheese. Bake for 7 to 10 minutes, or until the fish flakes easily with a fork.

NOTE: I like to serve this fish with buttered noodles that have been topped with a sprinkle of Parmesan cheese.

Creamy Sambuca Shrimp

4 to 5 servings

What a great unexpected combination of flavors. You've gotta taste it and see for yourself!

1 pound large shrimp, peeled
   and deveined, tails left on
¼ teaspoon salt
3 tablespoons butter
2 scallions, thinly sliced
2 plum tomatoes, thinly sliced

½ cup heavy cream
¼ cup sambuca (licorice-
   flavored liqueur)
2 tablespoons water
1 tablespoon all-purpose flour

Season the shrimp with the salt and set aside. In a large skillet, melt the butter over medium heat and sauté the scallions for 3 to 4 minutes, until tender. Add the shrimp and sauté for 3 to 4 minutes, just until pink. Stir in the tomatoes, cream, and liqueur. In a small bowl, combine the water and flour; stir until smooth, then add to the skillet and stir until thickened. Serve immediately.

NOTE: For a heartier meal, serve the shrimp over warm cooked linguine or your favorite pasta, or even yellow rice.

Tomato Cream-Crusted Fish

4 to 6 servings

Try this for a change of pace from the ordinary baked-on toppings. It's truly the cream of the crop!

1 package (3 ounces) cream
   cheese, softened
2 tablespoons tomato paste
½ teaspoon dried basil
½ teaspoon garlic powder
¼ teaspoon dried thyme

¼ teaspoon salt
⅛ teaspoon black pepper
2 pounds fresh or frozen
   white-fleshed fish fillets,
   such as cod, haddock, or
   whiting, thawed if frozen

Preheat the oven to 350°F. In a small bowl, combine all the ingredients except the fish; mix well. Place the fish on a rimmed baking sheet that has been coated with nonstick cooking spray. Spread the cream cheese mixture evenly over the top of the fish and bake for 18 to 20 minutes, or until the fish flakes easily with a fork.

NOTE: For more cheese flavor, add 1 to 2 tablespoons grated Parmesan cheese to the cream cheese mixture.

Garden-Fresh Baked Tuna

4 servings

Who said all tuna fish is the same? You won't need a can opener to enjoy the fresh tastes of both the garden and the ocean . . . at the same time!

2 tablespoons olive oil, divided
2 teaspoons balsamic vinegar
4 tuna steaks (about 1½
   pounds total), 1 inch thick
2 teaspoons dried rosemary

¼ teaspoon crushed red pepper
½ teaspoon salt
2 medium-sized plum
   tomatoes, chopped

Preheat the oven to 350°F. Sprinkle 1 tablespoon oil over the bottom of a 9″ × 13″ baking dish. Place the tuna in the baking dish and sprinkle with the remaining 1 tablespoon oil and the balsamic vinegar. Sprinkle the rosemary, red pepper, and salt evenly over the fish. Top with the tomatoes and bake for 18 to 20 minutes, or until the tuna is cooked to desired doneness.

NOTE: This is a perfect dish to make if you like your tuna steak medium-rare or even rare. Just make sure to use very fresh tuna, and reduce the cooking time to achieve the desired doneness.

Herb-Crusted Salmon

4 servings

In our family, we like to give a thumbs-up to a great meal. This one earns it for its tasty crunch!

1 cup mayonnaise	½ teaspoon dried basil
1 tablespoon grated Parmesan cheese	¼ teaspoon black pepper
½ teaspoon dried oregano	4 salmon fillets (about 1½ pounds total)

Preheat the oven to 425°F. In a medium-sized bowl, combine all the ingredients except the salmon; mix well. Place the salmon on a rimmed baking sheet that has been coated with nonstick cooking spray and spread the mayonnaise mixture evenly over the tops and sides of the fillets. Bake for 12 to 15 minutes, or until the salmon flakes easily with a fork and the topping is golden.

NOTE: This can be prepared ahead of time, but keep it refrigerated and bake just before serving, because the salmon is at its best right out of the oven.

Seafood Fra Diavolo

6 to 8 servings

Every Italian family has a recipe for this seafood lover's dish. And if you're one of the ones who really likes it hot, this is the one for you!

3 tablespoons olive oil
5 garlic cloves, coarsely
  chopped
1 can (28 ounces) crushed
  tomatoes, undrained
1 can (28 ounces) diced
  tomatoes, undrained
2 teaspoons dried oregano
1 teaspoon dried basil
1 teaspoon sugar

1 teaspoon crushed red pepper
1½ teaspoons salt
½ teaspoon black pepper
1 dozen littleneck clams,
  cleaned
2 pounds mussels, cleaned
  (see Note on page 40)
1 pound large shrimp, peeled
  and deveined
1 pound spaghetti

In a large pot, heat the oil over medium heat and sauté the garlic for 2 to 3 minutes, until golden. Stir in the crushed and diced tomatoes, the oregano, basil, sugar, red pepper, salt, and black pepper. Reduce the heat to medium-low, cover, and simmer for 25 to 30 minutes. Place the clams and mussels in the pot; cover and cook for 5 minutes. Add the shrimp and cook for 5 to 7 minutes, or until the clams and mussels have opened and the shrimp is pink. Meanwhile, cook the spaghetti according to the package directions and drain. **Discard any unopened clams or mussels** and serve the seafood and sauce over the spaghetti.

Italian Fish Cakes

4 to 6 servings

Ever since fish cakes and fish sticks found their way to the frozen food section of the supermarket, we've forgotten how good homemade can be. Here's a quick reminder.

1 can (7¾ ounces) garbanzo
    beans (chick peas), drained
1 can (8¾ ounces) whole
    kernel corn, drained
2 scallions, cut into 2-inch
    pieces
1 pound fresh or frozen white-
    fleshed fish fillets, such as
    cod, haddock, or whiting,
    thawed if frozen, cut into
    chunks

2 eggs
1¼ cups Italian-flavored bread
    crumbs, divided
½ cup grated Parmesan cheese
1 teaspoon Italian seasoning
½ teaspoon salt
½ teaspoon black pepper
Vegetable oil for frying

Place the garbanzo beans, corn, and scallions in a food processor that has been fitted with its metal cutting blade. Process for 10 to 15 seconds, until coarsely chopped. Add the fish and eggs and process for 10 to 15 seconds more, until the fish is chopped and the mixture is well blended; place in a large bowl. Add ½ cup bread crumbs, the Parmesan cheese, Italian seasoning, salt, and pepper. Using your hands, form the mixture into patties, using about ⅓ cup for each. Place the remaining ¾ cup bread crumbs in a shallow dish and coat the patties completely with the bread crumbs. Heat about ½ inch oil in a large deep skillet over medium heat until hot but not smoking. Cook the patties a few at a time for 3 to 4 minutes per side, until cooked through and golden, adding more oil if needed. Drain on paper towels.

NOTE: *Go ahead and make these in advance. Then all you need to do is warm them up on a baking sheet in a 300°F. oven for about 25 minutes, or until hot.*

Rice and Potatoes
Riso e Patate

Ready-in-Minutes Risotto

3 to 4 servings

You usually have to go through lots of steps, with lots of stirring, to make traditional risotto. Now it's as easy as 1–2–3!

2 tablespoons butter
1 cup long- or whole-grain rice
1 can (10½ ounces) condensed
  chicken broth

1 cup water
4 scallions, chopped
¼ cup grated Parmesan cheese

In a medium-sized saucepan, melt the butter over medium heat. Add the rice and sauté until golden. Add the chicken broth and bring to a boil. Reduce the heat to low, cover, and simmer for 10 minutes, stirring once. Add the water and scallions and return to a boil, then reduce the heat to low and simmer for 10 minutes, or until the rice is tender. Remove from the heat and stir in the cheese until blended. Serve immediately.

Asparagus Risotto

3 to 4 servings

No need to wait for the fresh springtime crop of asparagus! Nope—'cause the secret to the richness of this dish is in the can!

2 tablespoons butter
2 tablespoons olive oil
1 small onion, finely chopped
1 cup long- or whole-grain rice
1 can (14½ ounces) ready-to-use chicken broth
1 can (15 ounces) asparagus cuts, drained and mashed (see Note)
½ cup grated Parmesan cheese

In a medium-sized saucepan, heat the butter and oil over medium-high heat. Add the onion and cook for 4 to 5 minutes, or until golden. Add the rice and cook for 1 minute, stirring until the rice is coated. Add the broth and bring to a boil. Reduce the heat to low, cover, and simmer for 15 minutes. Add the asparagus, cover, and cook for 5 minutes. Add the Parmesan cheese and stir until the liquid is absorbed and the rice is creamy. Serve immediately.

NOTE: It's easy to mash the asparagus—just drain the liquid from the can and, with a fork, mash the asparagus right in the can.

Spicy Sausage Risotto

You don't have to be Italian to love this sausage-laced winner!!

1 tablespoon olive oil
1 pound bulk hot Italian
  sausage
1 small onion, finely diced
½ pound fresh mushrooms,
  quartered
1 can (14½ ounces) Italian-
  style stewed tomatoes,
  undrained

½ teaspoon garlic powder
2 cups long- or whole-
  grain rice
3 cups water
1 can (14½ ounces) ready-to-
  use beef broth
1 cup grated Parmesan cheese

In a large pot, heat the oil over medium heat. Add the sausage and onion and cook for 5 to 6 minutes, until no pink remains in the sausage, stirring to break up the sausage as it cooks. Add the mushrooms, tomatoes, and garlic powder and cook for 5 to 6 minutes, or until the mushrooms are tender. Add the rice, water, and broth. Cook, uncovered, for 25 to 30 minutes, or until the liquid is absorbed and the rice is tender. Stir in the Parmesan cheese until well blended. Serve immediately.

NOTE: This is enough for 6 to 8 as a side dish, but remember that it serves fewer as a main course.

Onion Risotto

6 to 8 servings

If you've ever thought rice was bland, you've never tasted it this way.

¼ cup (½ stick) butter
3 medium-sized onions, coarsely chopped
2 cups long- or whole-grain rice

3 cans (14½ ounces each) ready-to-use beef broth
1 cup grated Parmesan cheese

In a large skillet, melt the butter over medium-low heat. Add the onions and cook for 25 to 30 minutes, or until caramelized, stirring occasionally (see Note). Add the rice and stir for 1 minute, until coated with butter. Add the broth, increase the heat to medium, and cook for 25 to 30 minutes, or until the rice is tender and the liquid is absorbed. Add the Parmesan cheese and stir until well blended. Serve immediately.

NOTE: Don't worry that you'll cook the onions too much. Make sure they're completely caramelized before adding the rice.

Risotto with Fennel

6 to 8 servings

The bulb type of fennel has been used in Europe for centuries, but only recently has it become an American favorite. I can't imagine why it took so long to catch on!

¼ cup (½ stick) butter
1 small onion, diced
2 fennel bulbs, trimmed and
   diced (see Note)
2 cups long- or whole-
   grain rice
3 cups water

¾ cup dry white wine
¾ cup milk
1 teaspoon salt
½ teaspoon black pepper
2 tablespoons chopped fresh
   basil
1 cup grated Parmesan cheese

In a large pot, melt the butter over medium-low heat. Add the onion and fennel and sauté for 5 to 7 minutes, or until tender. Add the rice and stir to coat the rice with butter. Add the water, wine, milk, salt, and pepper, then cover and cook for 20 minutes, stirring occasionally. Uncover and continue to cook until all the liquid is absorbed and the rice is tender, stirring frequently. Stir in the basil and cheese until well blended. Serve immediately.

NOTE: A fennel bulb looks like a squatty celery bunch, with feathery dill-like leaves. To trim a fennel bulb, cut away the leafy green stems and stalks and trim the base of the bulb. You can use the leafy greens as a garnish, if you'd like.

Mushroom and Zucchini Risotto

6 to 8 servings

What a fresh-tasting variation of risotto—it's chock-full of tasty garden tidbits!

2 medium-sized onions, chopped
½ pound fresh mushrooms, sliced
2 teaspoons minced garlic
2 cups long- or whole-grain rice
1 medium-sized zucchini, coarsely shredded

1 can (14½ ounces) ready-to-use chicken broth
3 cups water
2 teaspoons Italian seasoning
½ teaspoon salt
¼ teaspoon black pepper
¾ cup grated Parmesan cheese

In a large saucepan that has been coated with nonstick cooking spray, sauté the onions, mushrooms, and garlic over medium-high heat for 5 to 7 minutes, or until the onions are tender. Add the rice and zucchini and cook for 3 to 5 minutes, or until the rice turns golden. Meanwhile, in a medium-sized saucepan, combine the chicken broth, water, Italian seasoning, salt, and pepper and bring to a boil over medium-high heat. Add the broth mixture to the rice, cover, and simmer over low heat for 15 minutes. Add the Parmesan cheese and stir for 1 to 2 minutes, until the mixture is creamy and well combined and all the liquid is absorbed. Serve immediately.

Spinach Pasta and Rice

4 to 6 servings

Bet you'll never guess what makes this super skillet side dish so good *and* good for you—why, this is probably one of Popeye's favorite ways with his favorite food . . . spinach!

2 tablespoons olive oil
½ cup mini ring pasta
   (see Note)
1 cup long- or whole-grain
   rice
1 package (10 ounces) frozen
   chopped spinach, thawed
   and well drained

2 cans (10½ ounces each)
   condensed chicken broth

In a large skillet, heat the oil over medium-high heat. Add the pasta and cook for 1 to 2 minutes, or until golden, stirring frequently. Stir in the remaining ingredients and bring to a boil. Reduce the heat to low, cover, and simmer for 20 to 25 minutes, or until all the liquid is absorbed and the rice is tender.

NOTE: Rings, orzo, or any type of miniature pasta can be used— even alphabet pasta, for an educational as well as tasty side dish.

Vegetable and Bacon Rice

6 to 8 servings

I think sometimes we get so used to enjoying bacon as a break-fast staple that we forget to use it as a flavoring. Well, just look what it does for *this* dish!

½ pound bacon, chopped
   (see Note)
1 small onion, chopped
2 cups long- or whole-grain
   rice, divided

2 cans (10½ ounces each)
   condensed chicken broth
1 package (16 ounces) frozen
   peas and carrots

In a large skillet, cook the bacon and onion over medium-high heat for 8 to 10 minutes, or until the bacon browns. Stir in 1 cup rice and cook for 4 to 5 minutes, or until the rice is golden and the bacon is crisp. Add the broth, the remaining 1 cup rice, and the peas and carrots; mix well. Bring to a boil, cover, and reduce the heat to low. Simmer for 20 to 25 minutes, or until the liquid is absorbed and the rice is tender.

NOTE: This dish is traditionally made with pancetta, which is from the same cut of meat used for bacon. Pancetta is salted, though, not smoked—but, really, any type of bacon will give this a great flavor.

Golden Polenta

6 to 8 servings

Polenta is so many things that I couldn't decide which chapter it fit best. Try it for a change instead of bread, as an antipasto, a snack, or even a main dish. Talk about a golden opportunity!

4 cups water	2 cups fine-ground yellow
¼ cup (½ stick) butter	cornmeal
1½ teaspoons salt	

Place the water, butter, and salt in a large saucepan and bring to a boil over high heat. Remove from the heat and slowly whisk in the cornmeal until the mixture is smooth and no lumps remain. Spoon the mixture into a 9″ × 5″ loaf pan that has been coated with nonstick cooking spray, packing it down firmly. Allow to cool for at least 1 hour, or until firm. Invert the pan over a cutting board to remove the polenta. Cut into thick slices and serve.

NOTE: Polenta can be served as is and can also be sautéed, grilled, and even deep-fried. It also makes a great base for grilled vegetables or chicken.

Snappy
Pesto-Onion Polenta

6 to 8 servings

Simple becomes jazzy when we add some spark to an all-around favorite. Better make a spare loaf—it'll be snapped right up!

4 cups water
¼ cup (½ stick) butter
2 teaspoons salt
2 cups fine-ground yellow
    cornmeal

½ cup prepared pesto sauce
1 can (2.8 ounces) French-fried
    onions

Place the water, butter, and salt in a large saucepan and bring to a boil over high heat. Remove from the heat and slowly whisk in the cornmeal until the mixture is smooth and no lumps remain. Whisk in the pesto until completely blended, then stir in the onions. Spoon the mixture into a 9″ × 5″ loaf pan that has been coated with nonstick cooking spray, packing it down firmly. Allow to cool for at least 1 hour, or until firm. Invert the pan over a cutting board to remove the polenta. Cut into thick slices and serve.

NOTE: The polenta slices can be rewarmed in the oven, panfried, or grilled before serving.

Potatoes Romana

These simple potatoes are full of flavor and provide the perfect balance for roasted meats or grilled fish.

2 tablespoons olive oil
4 medium-sized red potatoes (about 1¾ pounds total), cut into thin wedges (see Note)
½ of a sweet onion, thinly sliced
3 garlic cloves, chopped
1 teaspoon dried parsley flakes
½ teaspoon Italian seasoning
½ teaspoon salt
¼ teaspoon black pepper
2 tablespoons grated Romano cheese

In a large skillet, heat the oil over medium-high heat. Add the remaining ingredients except the cheese and sauté for 10 minutes. Reduce the heat to low, cover, and cook for 10 to 12 more minutes, or until the potatoes are tender. Sprinkle with the Romano cheese and serve.

NOTE: You could really use 1¾ pounds of almost any type of potatoes. You can peel them or not, and cut them into wedges, slices, or even chunks—the choice is up to you. Just try to make all the pieces uniform so they cook in the same amount of time.

Roasted Mashed Potatoes

I can almost guarantee that you've never had mashed potatoes quite like this before. Boy, the seasonings and little extras in here really make this a special dish!

6 medium-sized red potatoes (about 2½ pounds total), cut into 1-inch chunks
3 tablespoons olive oil
2 medium-sized onions, thinly sliced
1 jar (7 ounces) roasted red peppers, drained and chopped
1 medium-sized tomato, diced
3 garlic cloves, minced
1 tablespoon sugar
1 teaspoon Italian seasoning
1 cup milk
½ cup (1 stick) butter, softened
1 cup grated Parmesan cheese
1 teaspoon salt
½ teaspoon black pepper

Place the potatoes in a large pot and add just enough water to cover them. Bring to a boil over medium-high heat and cook for 20 to 25 minutes, or until tender. Meanwhile, in a large skillet, heat the oil over medium-high heat and sauté the onions for 4 to 5 minutes, or until tender. Add the roasted peppers, tomato, garlic, sugar, and Italian seasoning; sauté for 5 minutes, then set aside. Drain the potatoes and place in a large bowl. Add the milk, butter, Parmesan cheese, salt, and black pepper. Beat with an electric beater on medium speed for 2 to 3 minutes, or until smooth. Add the onion mixture and stir until well blended. Serve immediately.

NOTE: If you'd rather make this a bit before serving time, put it in a covered casserole dish and keep warm in a 300°F. oven until ready to serve.

Perfect Pesto Potatoes

4 to 6 servings

These are so easy, yet everyone will think you fussed for hours. What's the secret? Use prepared pesto sauce and let the oven do all the work!

⅓ cup prepared pesto sauce
½ teaspoon salt
¼ teaspoon black pepper

6 medium-sized baking potatoes (about 2½ pounds total), cut into 1-inch chunks

Preheat the oven to 425°F. In a large bowl, combine the pesto sauce, salt, and pepper; mix well. Add the potatoes and toss until well coated. Place the potatoes on a large rimmed baking sheet. Bake for 35 to 40 minutes, or until crisp and brown on the outside and tender on the inside, turning halfway through the baking.

NOTE: Why not sprinkle these with grated Parmesan cheese just before serving for extra cheesy flavor? I like to use potatoes with the skin on, but if you prefer, you can peel them first.

Italian Stuffed Baked Potatoes

6 servings

Stuffed potatoes are so popular these days that it's getting tough to serve them and be different from everybody else. Well, you just try fixing them this way and see how far from ordinary they'll be!

6 large baking potatoes
½ cup (1 stick) butter
1 medium-sized red or green bell pepper, finely chopped (see Note)
1 small onion, chopped
1 garlic clove, minced
1 teaspoon salt
¼ teaspoon black pepper
1 container (15 ounces) ricotta cheese
¼ cup grated Parmesan cheese

Preheat the oven to 400°F. Scrub the potatoes and pierce the skins several times with a fork. Bake for 55 to 60 minutes, or until tender. Meanwhile, in a large skillet, melt the butter over medium-high heat and add the bell pepper, onion, garlic, salt, and black pepper; sauté for 6 to 8 minutes, or until the onion is golden. Remove from the heat and set aside. Slice about 1 inch off the top of each potato and spoon out the insides; place the pulp in a large bowl. Add the onion mixture and the ricotta and Parmesan cheeses and beat with an electric beater until well blended. Spoon into the potato shells and place on a baking sheet; bake for 20 to 30 minutes, or until the potatoes are heated through and golden.

NOTE: I like to use half of a green bell pepper and half of a red bell pepper to make a very colorful stuffing.

Special Roasted Potatoes

4 to 6 servings

Even when we're not in Rome, it pays to do what the Romans do—at least when it comes to the seasonings and little extras that can really make a dish special!

¼ cup olive oil
2 tablespoons chopped fresh
  basil
1 tablespoon minced garlic
2 teaspoons dried oregano
1 teaspoon salt
¼ teaspoon black pepper
3 large red potatoes (about
  1¼ pounds total), cut into
  ¼-inch slices

2 medium-sized bell peppers
  (1 red and 1 green), cut into
  1-inch strips
3 ripe tomatoes, cut into
  wedges

Preheat the oven to 450°F. In a large bowl, combine the oil, basil, garlic, oregano, salt, and black pepper. Add the potatoes, bell peppers, and tomatoes and toss until coated and well mixed. Spoon the mixture into a 9″ × 13″ baking dish that has been coated with nonstick cooking spray and bake for 40 to 45 minutes, or until the vegetables are tender.

NOTE: Feel free to add your favorite vegetables, including sliced eggplant or portobello mushrooms, or even yellow or orange bell peppers.

241

Vegetables
Verdure

Golden Cauliflower Bake

4 to 6 servings

Oven-crispy and so simple! All we do here is give our cauliflower lots of flavor with everyday seasonings and bake it to perfection. Like that, don't you?!

½ cup olive oil
1 cup Italian-flavored bread crumbs
1 teaspoon garlic powder
¼ teaspoon salt
¼ teaspoon black pepper
2 packages (10 ounces each) frozen cauliflower florets, thawed
Nonstick cooking spray

Preheat the oven to 400°F. Place the oil in a small bowl. Place the bread crumbs, garlic powder, salt, and pepper in another small bowl. Dip each cauliflower floret into the oil, then into the bread crumb mixture. Place in an 8-inch square baking dish that has been coated with nonstick cooking spray. Coat the breaded florets with nonstick cooking spray and bake for 20 to 25 minutes, or until light golden.

NOTE: This can also be made with fresh cauliflower. Just cut it into florets and steam or boil until tender, then proceed as above.

Sicilian Zucchini

We don't have to wait for a special occasion to dress up this popular squash. We can perk it up any day . . . the Sicilian way!

2 tablespoons olive oil	½ cup Italian-flavored bread
6 medium-sized zucchini,	crumbs
coarsely chopped	1 can (10½ ounces) condensed
1 medium-sized onion,	chicken broth
chopped	¼ teaspoon salt
2 garlic cloves, minced	¼ teaspoon black pepper

In a large skillet, heat the oil over medium-high heat and sauté the zucchini for 5 minutes. Add the onion and garlic and cook for 5 to 7 more minutes, or until the vegetables are tender. Add the bread crumbs and sauté for 3 to 5 minutes, or until the bread crumbs are golden. Stir in the remaining ingredients, reduce the heat to medium-low, cover, and simmer for 12 to 15 minutes, or until the vegetables are very tender.

NOTE: You know this is done when the zucchini is almost falling apart.

Broccoli Rabe Sauté

Who would have guessed that something as simple as this veggie dish could be so . . . well, as they say in Italy, *"Magnifico!"*

¼ cup olive oil, divided
1 bunch broccoli rabe, trimmed
½ cup chicken broth

4 garlic cloves, minced
¼ teaspoon salt
¼ teaspoon black pepper

Heat the oil in a large skillet over medium-high heat. Reduce the heat to medium-low and place the broccoli rabe in the skillet. Cover and cook for 20 minutes, stirring occasionally. Stir in the remaining ingredients and cook for 8 to 10 minutes, or until the broccoli rabe is tender.

NOTE: Serve with lemon wedges for squeezing over the top just before eating. To turn this into a great vegetarian main course, during the last 8 to 10 minutes of cooking, add a can of Great Northern beans and a dash of crushed red pepper. It's a dish that's fast becoming popular all around the country.

Saucy Green Beans

4 to 6 servings

There's nothing wrong with plain freshly steamed green beans, but it's hard to go back to them after trying these!

1 package (16 ounces) frozen cut green beans (see Note)
2 cups spaghetti sauce
1 tablespoon olive oil
1 teaspoon minced garlic
½ teaspoon salt
¼ teaspoon black pepper

Place the green beans in a large saucepan and add just enough water to cover them. Bring to a boil over high heat and cook for 5 to 7 minutes, or until tender. Drain the beans and return to the saucepan. Add the remaining ingredients; mix well. Reduce the heat to medium-low, cover, and simmer for 5 minutes, stirring frequently. Serve immediately.

NOTE: If you prefer to use fresh green beans, trim 1½ pounds of beans and cut in half; they'll have to boil a bit longer before they're tender. And go ahead and make these Parmesan Green Beans by sprinkling with grated Parmesan cheese just before serving.

Broccoli Italiano

The flavoring of this one will make broccoli lovers out of your whole gang. It's a guaranteed hit, and it couldn't be easier!

1 bunch broccoli, cut into spears	⅔ cup Italian dressing
	⅓ cup dry white wine

In a large skillet, combine all the ingredients. Cover and simmer for 12 to 15 minutes, or until the broccoli is tender.

NOTE: For added flavor and color, add a finely chopped red bell pepper to the skillet with the other ingredients.

Seasoned Stuffed Tomatoes

6 servings

Team a tomato with the right "stuff" and it'll go a long way with its great taste!

3 large tomatoes, cut in half crosswise and seeded (see Note)
¾ cup Italian-flavored bread crumbs

¼ cup grated Parmesan cheese
⅛ teaspoon black pepper
¼ cup (½ stick) butter, melted
1 teaspoon Dijon-style mustard

Preheat the oven to 350°F. With a spoon, scoop out the insides of the tomatoes, leaving the shells. Finely chop the tomato pulp and set aside. In a medium-sized bowl, combine the bread crumbs, cheese, and pepper; mix well. Add the chopped tomato pulp, butter, and mustard; mix until well combined. Fill the tomato shells evenly with the stuffing mixture and place in a 7″ × 11″ baking dish that has been coated with nonstick cooking spray. Bake for 30 to 35 minutes, or until the tomatoes are heated through and the topping is light golden.

NOTE: To seed the tomatoes, gently squeeze each half until the seeds are released.

Potato and Fennel Bake

4 to 6 servings

The first thing most of us think of when we hear fennel is fennel seed. But many recipes use the bulb type of fennel. And using it in bulb form is a whole different (still flavorful!) ball game, as you'll discover when you taste this one.

2 tablespoons olive oil
1 fennel bulb, trimmed and coarsely chopped (see Note on page 231)
6 scallions, chopped
1 can (10¾ ounces) condensed cream of potato soup
½ cup milk
¼ cup plus 2 tablespoons grated Parmesan cheese
2 cans (15 ounces each) sliced potatoes, drained
2 tablespoons plain dry bread crumbs

Preheat the oven to 350°F. In a large skillet, heat the oil over medium heat and sauté the fennel and scallions for 12 to 15 minutes, or until the fennel is tender; set aside. In a large bowl, combine the soup, milk, and ¼ cup Parmesan cheese. Add the potatoes and the fennel mixture and toss to combine. Spoon the mixture into an 8-inch square baking dish that has been coated with nonstick cooking spray. Sprinkle with the bread crumbs and the remaining 2 tablespoons Parmesan cheese and bake for 25 to 30 minutes, or until warmed through.

Zucchini Boats

6 servings

Want to get the kids to beg you for veggies? Make your vegetables look and taste like this clever little stuffed treat and they'll gobble them up!

3 medium-sized zucchini, sliced in half lengthwise
2 tablespoons olive oil
1 can (4 ounces) mushroom stems and pieces, drained and chopped
1 small onion, chopped
2 plum tomatoes, diced

¼ cup Italian-flavored bread crumbs
1 tablespoon grated Parmesan cheese
½ teaspoon salt
¼ teaspoon black pepper
½ cup (2 ounces) shredded mozzarella cheese

Preheat the oven to 375°F. With a spoon, scoop the pulp out of the zucchini halves, leaving ¼ inch of meat around the edges; set aside the shells and chop the zucchini pulp finely. In a medium-sized skillet, heat the oil over medium heat and sauté the chopped zucchini, mushrooms, onion, and tomatoes for 6 to 8 minutes, or until tender. Stir in the bread crumbs, Parmesan cheese, salt, and pepper until well mixed. Stuff the zucchini shells evenly with the vegetable mixture and place in a 9" × 13" baking dish that has been coated with nonstick cooking spray. Cover tightly with aluminum foil and bake for 35 minutes. Remove the foil and top evenly with the mozzarella cheese. Bake for 8 to 10 minutes, or until the zucchini is tender and the cheese is golden.

Garlicky Sautéed Spinach

4 servings

There's no need to bribe the kids to eat their spinach—at least not when you dish it up this way. In fact, you may have to beg them to leave some for you!

3 tablespoons olive oil
2 tablespoons chopped garlic
2 packages (10 ounces each)
fresh spinach, trimmed and
washed but not dried

¼ cup dry white wine
1 teaspoon salt
1 teaspoon black pepper

Heat the oil over medium-high heat in a large pot and sauté the garlic for 3 to 4 minutes, or until golden. Stir in the spinach, wine, salt, and pepper and reduce the heat to low. Cover and simmer for 5 to 6 minutes, or just until the spinach wilts completely. Serve immediately.

NOTE: When spinach cooks, it reduces much of its bulk, so that's why this makes just 4 servings.

Orzo-Stuffed Peppers

6 servings

A lot of people use bread crumbs in their stuffed peppers, but sometimes it's nice to get a change of texture . . . and orzo pasta offers just the right variation.

1 pound ground beef
1 cup uncooked orzo pasta
1 can (29 ounces) tomato
   sauce, divided
1 teaspoon dried basil
1 teaspoon garlic powder

1 teaspoon salt
½ teaspoon black pepper
6 medium-sized green bell
   peppers, tops removed,
   cored, and seeded
½ cup water

In a large bowl, combine the ground beef, orzo, 1½ cups tomato sauce, the basil, garlic powder, salt, and black pepper; mix well. Stuff the bell peppers evenly with the mixture. Stand the peppers in a large pot and pour the remaining tomato sauce over the top. Pour the water into the bottom of the pot, cover, and cook over medium-low heat for 50 to 60 minutes, or until the meat is cooked and the peppers are tender.

NOTE: For extra color, add a finely chopped red bell pepper to the ground beef mixture.

Asparagus Parmigiana

4 to 6 servings

When I want a special side dish with practically no work, this is definitely on my top-ten list.

2 cups spaghetti sauce
2 packages (10 ounces each)
   frozen asparagus spears or
   cuts, thawed (see Note)

1 cup (4 ounces) shredded
   mozzarella cheese

Preheat the oven to 350°F. Spread 1 cup spaghetti sauce over the bottom of an 8-inch square baking dish that has been coated with nonstick cooking spray. Lay the asparagus in the sauce and top with the remaining 1 cup sauce. Sprinkle with the cheese and bake for 35 to 40 minutes, or until heated through.

NOTE: In the spring, when fresh asparagus is so abundant, I steam a bunch or two until tender and use it in this recipe instead of the frozen asparagus.

Greens and Beans

4 to 6 servings

This Italian specialty is a worldwide favorite. And what a combo it is! If you've never tried greens and beans, you're in for a treat.

3 tablespoons olive oil
½ of a medium-sized onion, chopped
3 garlic cloves, minced
½ teaspoon Italian seasoning
½ teaspoon crushed red pepper

½ teaspoon salt
1 can (15½ ounces) Great Northern beans, undrained
1 head escarole, washed, drained, and coarsely chopped

In a large pot, heat the oil over medium heat. Add the onion, garlic, Italian seasoning, crushed red pepper, and salt and sauté for 2 to 3 minutes, or until the onion is tender. Add half of the beans, then mash the remaining beans in the can with a fork. Add the mashed beans to the pot and cook for 3 minutes. Add the escarole and cook for 5 minutes, until slightly wilted, stirring frequently. Reduce the heat to low, cover, and simmer for 8 to 10 minutes, or until the escarole is tender. Serve immediately.

NOTE: If you'd prefer, cannellini (white kidney beans) or even garbanzo beans (chick peas) can be substituted for the Great Northern beans. Use whatever you like best.

Broccoli-Mushroom Bake

4 to 6 servings

No need to wait for company to turn out fancy-looking, taste-tempting side dishes. This way it's a snap to make the gang at home feel special . . . any day of the week.

2 packages (10 ounces each) frozen broccoli spears, thawed and drained (see Note)
⅛ teaspoon black pepper
1 can (10¾ ounces) condensed cream of mushroom soup

¼ cup milk
¼ cup grated Parmesan cheese
¼ cup Italian-flavored bread crumbs

Preheat the oven to 350°F. Place the broccoli spears in a single layer in an 8-inch square baking dish that has been coated with nonstick cooking spray; sprinkle with the pepper. In a small bowl, mix together the soup and milk and pour evenly over the broccoli. Sprinkle with the Parmesan cheese and bread crumbs. Bake for 35 to 40 minutes, or until warmed through and golden on top.

NOTE: This can also be made with fresh broccoli that you cut into spears and boil or steam until tender.

Vegetable Frittata

6 to 8 servings

Somewhere between a soufflé and a pudding is the baked frittata. But you can bet it won't be there long!

6 eggs
½ cup milk
½ cup grated Parmesan cheese
½ cup (2 ounces) shredded
    mozzarella cheese

½ teaspoon salt
½ teaspoon black pepper
1 package (16 ounces) frozen
    Italian mixed vegetables,
    thawed and drained

Preheat the oven to 350°F. In a medium-sized bowl, beat the eggs and milk with a fork until well combined. Beat in the Parmesan and mozzarella cheeses, the salt, and pepper; stir in the vegetables. Pour the mixture into an 8-inch square baking dish that has been coated with nonstick cooking spray. Bake for 40 to 45 minutes, until the top is golden brown and the center is set. Remove from the oven and allow to sit for 5 minutes before cutting and serving.

NOTE: This can be made ahead and chilled or even frozen until ready to reheat and serve.

Desserts
Dolci

continued

Tiramisù

6 to 8 servings

Tiramisù means "pick me up," and who wouldn't want to pick up a forkful of this creamy pick-me-up!

1 cup warm water	½ cup refrigerated egg
4 teaspoons instant coffee	substitute
granules	½ cup sugar
¼ cup coffee-flavored liqueur	1 cup (½ pint) heavy cream
1 container (8 ounces)	2 packages (3 ounces each)
mascarpone cheese	ladyfingers
(see page xxi)	½ teaspoon unsweetened cocoa

In a small bowl, combine the water, coffee granules, and coffee liqueur; stir to dissolve the coffee, then set aside. In a large bowl, with an electric beater on medium speed, blend the cheese, egg substitute, and sugar until smooth; set aside. In a medium-sized bowl, with an electric beater on medium speed, beat the heavy cream until stiff peaks form. Fold half of the whipped cream into the cheese mixture until thoroughly mixed. Using one package of ladyfingers, quickly dip the ladyfingers into the coffee mixture one at a time and line the bottom of an 8-inch square baking dish. Spoon half of the cheese mixture evenly over the ladyfingers. Dip the remaining package of ladyfingers into the coffee mixture one at a time and place evenly over the cheese layer; top with the remaining cheese mixture. Spoon the remaining whipped cream over the top and sprinkle with the cocoa. Cover and chill for at least 3 hours before serving.

Little Italy Cheesecake

8 to 10 servings

I'm a big cheesecake fan, and I always tended to lean toward ones rich in cream cheese. Well, that was until I found this lower-fat ricotta-filled alternative.

¾ cup graham cracker crumbs
2 tablespoons butter, melted
1 container (15 ounces) part-
  skim ricotta cheese
1 cup plain low-fat yogurt
¾ cup sugar

2 tablespoons all-purpose flour
2 tablespoons lemon juice
1 package (8 ounces) reduced-
  fat cream cheese, softened
2 eggs
2½ teaspoons vanilla extract

Preheat the oven to 350°F. In a small bowl, combine the graham cracker crumbs and melted butter; press into the bottom and up the sides of a 9-inch deep-dish glass pie plate. Bake for 3 to 5 minutes, until lightly browned; let cool. (Leave the oven on.) In a large bowl, with an electric beater on medium speed, combine the ricotta cheese, yogurt, sugar, flour, and lemon juice until smooth; set aside. In another large bowl, with an electric beater on medium speed, beat the cream cheese, eggs, and vanilla until thoroughly combined. Add the ricotta mixture, beating on low speed until well combined. Pour into the pie crust and bake for 60 to 65 minutes, or until the center is nearly set. Cool for 30 to 45 minutes, then refrigerate overnight before serving.

NOTE: Why not top this with fresh strawberry slices or whole blueberries or raspberries?

Chocolate Hazelnut Cake

12 to 16 servings

If you make this for someone's birthday, you can be sure that when he or she blows out the candles, the wish will be for you to make it *every* year!

1 package (18½ ounces) chocolate cake mix
1 cup water
⅓ cup vegetable oil
3 eggs
⅔ cup chocolate-hazelnut spread, divided

1 cup chopped hazelnuts, divided
½ cup (1 stick) butter, softened
3 cups confectioners' sugar
¼ cup milk

Preheat the oven to 350°F. In a large bowl, with an electric beater on medium speed, combine the cake mix, water, oil, eggs, ⅓ cup chocolate-hazelnut spread, and ½ cup hazelnuts until well blended. Pour the batter into two 9-inch round cake pans that have been coated with nonstick cooking spray. Bake for 30 to 35 minutes, or until a wooden toothpick inserted in the center comes out clean. Allow to cool slightly, then remove to a wire rack to cool completely. In a medium-sized bowl, with an electric beater on medium speed, combine the butter, confectioners' sugar, milk, and the remaining ⅓ cup chocolate-hazelnut spread until smooth. Place one cake layer upside down on a cake platter. Spread the top with some of the frosting. Place the second cake layer right side up on top of the first cake layer. Spread the top and sides evenly with the remaining frosting. Sprinkle the remaining ½ cup chopped hazelnuts over the top and serve, or cover and chill until ready to serve.

Italian Layer Cake

12 to 16 servings

We've all seen those huge fancy cakes at Italian restaurants—you know which ones I mean, the ones that have a bunch of cake layers oozing with whipped cream and cherries. They're like Italian trifle, and this one's laced with rum and almonds. Now we can put it on our dessert menu at home.

1 package (18½ ounces) yellow cake mix, batter prepared according to the package directions
1 package (4-serving size) instant vanilla pudding and pie filling, prepared according to the package directions
2 tablespoons unsweetened cocoa
¼ cup water
¼ cup light or dark rum
¼ cup sugar
1 can (21 ounces) cherry pie filling, divided
2 cups frozen whipped topping, thawed
1 cup chopped almonds

Preheat the oven to 350°F. Divide the cake batter evenly among three 8-inch cake pans that have been coated with nonstick cooking spray. Bake for 18 to 20 minutes, or until a wooden toothpick inserted in the center comes out clean. Allow to cool slightly, then remove to a wire rack to cool completely. Divide the prepared pudding evenly between 2 small bowls and add the cocoa to one bowl; stir until well blended, making chocolate pudding. In another small bowl, combine the water, rum, and sugar; stir until the sugar dissolves. Pour the rum mixture evenly over the cake layers. Place 1 cake layer upside down on a serving platter and top with the vanilla pudding and one third of the cherry pie filling. Place the second cake layer upside down over the pie filling and top with the chocolate pudding and half of the remaining cherry pie filling. Place the third cake layer upside down over the filling and spoon the remaining pie filling into the center. Frost the sides and the top of the cake, around the cherry pie filling, with the whipped topping. Sprinkle the chopped almonds over the whipped topping and chill for 2 hours. Serve, or cover and keep chilled until ready to serve.

Tiramisù Cake

12 to 16 servings

This popular ladyfinger-based dessert is even more special in cake form! Save room for seconds . . . and thirds!

1¾ cups water
½ cup light or dark rum
¾ cup sugar, divided
2 tablespoons instant espresso
   or coffee granules
1 package (18½ ounces) yellow
   cake mix
3 eggs
⅓ cup vegetable oil

1 container (8 ounces)
   mascarpone cheese
   (see page xxi)
2 cups frozen whipped topping,
   thawed
1 package (3 ounces)
   ladyfingers, split
½ teaspoon unsweetened cocoa

Preheat the oven to 350°F. In a small bowl, combine the water, rum, ¼ cup sugar, and the espresso granules; mix until the sugar and espresso are dissolved. In a large bowl, with an electric beater on medium speed, beat the cake mix, eggs, oil, and 1¼ cups of the rum mixture until smooth; reserve the remaining rum mixture. Pour the batter into two 9-inch round cake pans that have been coated with nonstick cooking spray. Bake for 25 to 30 minutes, or until a wooden toothpick inserted in the center comes out clean. Allow to cool slightly, then remove to a wire rack to cool completely. In a medium-sized bowl, with an electric beater on medium speed, beat the mascarpone cheese and the remaining ½ cup sugar for 3 to 4 minutes, until smooth. Place one cake layer upside down on a serving platter; prick the top several times with a fork. Pour half of the reserved rum mixture over the top; it will be absorbed into the cake. Spread the mascarpone mixture evenly over the cake layer, then place the second cake layer right side up over the cheese mixture. Prick the top of the second cake layer several times with a fork and pour the remaining rum mixture over the top; it will be absorbed into the cake. Frost the sides and top of the cake with the whipped topping. Place the split ladyfingers around the sides of the cake, standing on end and with the flat sides pressing into the frosting. Sprinkle the top with the cocoa and chill for 2 hours. Serve, or cover and keep chilled until ready to serve.

Baba au Rhum

12 babas

When you look at this ingredient list, don't be alarmed by the amount of rum it calls for. This European favorite is featured in Italian pastry shops throughout the world, and we've turned it into a quick-and-easy treat, thanks to packaged cake and pudding mixes.

1 package (18½ ounces) yellow cake mix, batter prepared according to the package directions
1 package (4-serving size) instant vanilla pudding and pie filling

1½ cups cold milk
2 cups water
2 cups sugar
1 cup light rum
1 cup frozen whipped topping, thawed
12 maraschino cherries

Preheat the oven to 350°F. Bake the batter according to the package directions for 1 dozen cupcakes, without paper liners; let cool. Meanwhile, in a medium-sized bowl, whisk the pudding mix and

Cut cupcakes halfway

Spoon in pudding

and top with whipped topping

milk for 1 to 2 minutes, or until thickened. Cover the pudding and chill. In a small bowl, combine the water, sugar, and rum, stirring until the sugar is dissolved; set aside. When the cupcakes have cooled completely, place them in a 9" × 13" baking dish. Slowly pour the rum mixture over the tops, allowing the liquid to soak into the cupcakes. Cover and chill for 1 to 2 hours. Remove the cupcakes from the rum mixture and place upside down on a serving platter. Using a knife, make 2 cuts halfway through each cupcake, forming an X. Spoon the pudding evenly over the cuts in each cupcake, opening up the cupcakes a bit. Top each with a dollop of whipped topping and a cherry. Serve, or cover and chill until ready to serve.

Bakery-Style Cannoli

8 cannoli

I can still see myself as a little boy gazing in the window of the Italian bakery and eyeing all the pretty pastries. When I was allowed to pick just one, which one was it? A cannoli, of course!

¾ cup confectioners' sugar
1 container (15 ounces) ricotta
   cheese
1 teaspoon vanilla extract

½ cup mini semisweet
   chocolate chips
⅛ teaspoon ground cinnamon
8 cannoli shells

In a large bowl, combine the confectioners' sugar, ricotta cheese, and vanilla until well blended. Stir in the chocolate chips and cinnamon until thoroughly combined. Spoon the filling into the cannoli shells (see Note). Serve, or cover and chill until ready to serve.

NOTE: For an easy way to fill the cannoli shells, place the ricotta cheese mixture in a resealable plastic storage bag. Snip off a corner of the bag with scissors and squeeze the mixture into the shells. For a fancier touch, dip the ends of the filled cannoli in chocolate sprinkles.

Italian Honey Balls

3 to 4 servings

No Christmas or other traditional celebration would be complete without these candylike *struffoli* cookies.

1 cup water	2 eggs
½ cup vegetable oil	½ cup honey
¼ teaspoon salt	½ cup sugar
1 cup all-purpose flour	⅛ teaspoon ground cinnamon

Preheat the oven to 400°F. In a medium-sized saucepan, bring the water, oil, and salt to a boil over high heat. Reduce the heat to low and slowly stir in the flour, beating with a wooden spoon until the mixture forms a ball; remove from the heat. Beat in the eggs one at a time until well blended and smooth. Using a ½-teaspoon measuring spoon, form the mixture into small balls and place about 1 inch apart on an ungreased cookie sheet. Bake for 25 to 30 minutes, or until golden; let cool. In a small saucepan, bring the honey, sugar, and cinnamon to a boil over medium-high heat. Continue boiling, stirring occasionally, until the sugar is completely dissolved. Remove from the heat and allow to cool slightly. Place the baked balls in a medium-sized bowl, add the honey mixture, and stir gently until the balls are completely coated. Pile the balls into a mound on a serving platter. Do not refrigerate.

NOTE: You can make this really festive by garnishing it with candied cherries, almonds, or even multicolored Jordan almonds (candy-coated almonds, also called "wedding confetti").

Fig and Walnut Truffles

about 48 truffles

A tin of these little wonders makes one of the sweetest gifts you could ever offer.

¾ cup heavy cream
6 tablespoons (¾ stick) butter
3 tablespoons light corn syrup
2 cups (12 ounces) semisweet
   chocolate chips

⅔ cup chopped figs
⅔ cup chopped toasted
   walnuts
2 tablespoons unsweetened
   cocoa

In a medium-sized saucepan, bring the cream, butter, and corn syrup to a boil over medium-low heat. Immediately remove from the heat and stir in the chocolate chips. Stir until the chocolate is completely melted and well combined, then stir in the figs and walnuts. Pour into an 8-inch square baking pan. Cover and chill for 1 to 2 hours, or until firm but not solid. Using a teaspoon, form the mixture into walnut-sized balls. Place the cocoa in a shallow dish and roll the truffles in the cocoa, coating completely. Place on a platter, then cover and chill for at least 2 hours, or until firm. Keep refrigerated.

NOTE: Instead of cocoa, you can roll the truffles in confectioners' sugar, if you'd like.

Sesame Cookies

about 60 cookies

Here's another crunchy cookie in the true Italian tradition—great for anytime munching and dunking.

1½ cups sugar	1 tablespoon honey
1 cup vegetable shortening	1 teaspoon vanilla extract
2 eggs	1 teaspoon grated lemon peel
3 cups all-purpose flour	¼ teaspoon salt
¼ cup milk	1½ cups sesame seeds

Preheat the oven to 350°F. In a large bowl, with an electric beater on medium speed, blend the sugar, shortening, and eggs until smooth. Add the flour, milk, honey, vanilla, lemon peel, and salt; stir until smooth, then set aside. Place the sesame seeds in a shallow bowl. Drop the dough by rounded teaspoonfuls into the sesame seeds and roll to coat. Shape into oblong cookies, each about 1″ × 2″, and place 1 inch apart on baking sheets that have been coated with nonstick cooking spray. Bake for 20 to 25 minutes, or until golden brown.

Rainbow Cookies

48 cookies

What's at the end of the rainbow? A plateful of colorful cookies that look just like these! (And they're a breeze to make, too!)

1½ teaspoons almond extract
1 package (18½ ounces) yellow cake mix, batter prepared according to the package directions
1 teaspoon red food color
1 teaspoon green food color
1 teaspoon yellow food color
1 jar (12 ounces) raspberry jam, melted
1 cup (6 ounces) semisweet chocolate chips, melted

Preheat the oven to 325°F. Stir the almond extract into the cake batter and divide the batter evenly among 3 small bowls. Stir the red food color into one bowl, the green food color into another bowl, and the yellow food color into the third bowl. Coat three 9″ × 13″ rimmed baking sheets with nonstick cooking spray, line with waxed paper, and coat again with nonstick cooking spray (see Note). Pour each colored batter onto a separate baking sheet and bake for 15 to 18 minutes, or until a wooden toothpick inserted in the center comes out clean; let cool completely. Invert the red layer onto a cutting board and remove the waxed paper. Spread half of the raspberry jam evenly over the top, then unmold the yellow cake and place upside down on top of the jam. Remove the waxed paper and spread the remaining jam over the yellow layer. Unmold the green cake layer and place upside down on top, leaving the waxed paper in place. Place a baking sheet on top to press the layers together. Chill for 1 hour, then remove from the refrigerator and remove the waxed paper. Spread the melted chocolate in a thin layer over the top and allow to harden slightly. Cut into 1″ × 2″ cookies and serve, or cover and chill until ready to serve.

NOTE: If you don't happen to have three 9″ × 13″ baking sheets, you can use 9″ × 13″ baking dishes; if you have only one, make the cake layers one at a time.

chocolate topping
green cake
raspberry jam
yellow cake
raspberry jam
red cake

RAINBOW COOKIES

CROSS SECTION

Italian Dippers

If these cookies could talk, they'd say, "Dunk me!" again and again.

4 eggs	2 cups all-purpose flour
1 cup sugar	2 teaspoons baking powder
4 teaspoons anise extract	⅛ teaspoon salt

Preheat the oven to 350°F. In a large bowl, cream the eggs and sugar. Add the anise extract. Slowly beat in the flour, baking powder, and salt until smooth and creamy. Drop the batter by teaspoonfuls into oblong shapes about 2 inches apart onto cookie sheets that have been coated with nonstick cooking spray. Bake for 8 to 10 minutes, or until golden.

NOTE: Place these cookies in an airtight container and they should last for weeks.

Featherlight Chocolate Drops

about 48 cookies

Craving something sweet? These are light as a feather and really hit the spot!

4 egg whites	1 teaspoon vanilla extract
2½ cups confectioners' sugar	1 cup chopped almonds
¾ cup unsweetened cocoa	

Preheat the oven to 325°F. In a medium-sized bowl, with an electric beater on medium-high speed, beat the egg whites until stiff peaks form. Add the sugar and beat until thick and glossy-looking. Fold in the cocoa and vanilla, then fold in the nuts until well blended. Drop the dough by rounded teaspoonfuls about 1 inch apart onto large baking sheets that have been lightly coated with nonstick cooking spray. Bake for 15 to 18 minutes, or until firm.

NOTE: It's a great holiday cookie, especially for Passover, or any-time you feel like a special treat—and it's so easy!

Cappuccino Dessert

4 to 6 servings

A few years ago, most Americans had never even heard of cappuccino. Now it's on everybody's lips—and in their coffee cups, too. Mmm!

2 cups cold milk
2 tablespoons instant coffee
  granules
1 package (4-serving size)
  instant chocolate pudding
  and pie filling

1½ cups frozen whipped
  topping, thawed
⅛ teaspoon ground cinnamon

In a large bowl, combine the milk and coffee granules. Add the pudding mix and beat with a wire whisk for 1 to 2 minutes, or until well blended. Put 2 tablespoons of the pudding into a medium-sized bowl and divide the remaining pudding among 4 coffee cups or 4 to 6 individual glass dessert dishes. Mix the whipped topping with the reserved pudding and spoon the topping mixture over the individual servings of pudding. Sprinkle the tops with the cinnamon and chill for at least 2 hours before serving.

NOTE: To really fool your gang, place this dessert in glass coffee mugs. That way, they'll really think it's a cappuccino drink.

Italian Cheese Pie

8 to 10 servings

What's the best way to make a classic Italian cheese pie? That's easy—use a classic Italian cheese!

6 eggs
½ cup sugar
½ teaspoon vanilla extract
2½ cups ricotta cheese

2 teaspoons grated lemon peel
1 unbaked 9-inch deep-dish pie
   shell

Preheat the oven to 350°F. In a large bowl, with an electric beater on medium speed, beat the eggs, sugar, vanilla, cheese, and lemon peel until well blended. Pour into the pie shell and bake for 65 to 70 minutes, or until the filling is set and the edges are golden. Let cool, then chill for 4 hours; serve, or cover and keep chilled until ready to serve.

NOTE: Don't worry if the center of the pie falls slightly after you take it out of the oven—mine usually does (and it still tastes great).

Italian Plum Tart

10 to 12 servings

If you're "plum"-ready for a sweet surprise, try out this tempting treat! And look—only four ingredients and you're on your way.

1 package (18 ounces) refrigerated sugar cookie dough
1 package (4-serving size) instant vanilla pudding and pie filling

1½ cups cold milk
6 Italian plums, pitted and cut into wedges (see Note)

Preheat the oven to 350°F. Coat a 12-inch pizza pan with non-stick cooking spray. Using your hands, roll the cookie dough into a ball and press evenly into the pizza pan, pressing the dough out to the edges of the pan; flour your hands if the dough becomes too sticky. Bake for 12 to 14 minutes, or until golden brown; let cool. In a medium-sized bowl, whisk the pudding mix and milk for 1 to 2 minutes, or until thickened. Chill for 15 to 20 minutes, then spread the pudding over the cooled cookie crust. Arrange the plum wedges evenly over the top and serve, or cover and keep chilled until ready to serve.

NOTE: If Italian plums aren't in season, any type of plum will do. Oh—Italian plums are an oval-shaped deep purple late-summer fruit.

Marsala Poached Pears

4 servings

With fresh pears readily available at any time of the year, this elegant dessert can be served up in no time whenever you want to make a great impression.

¾ cup sugar	½ cup sweet Marsala wine
⅔ cup water	4 pears, peeled

In a large saucepan, combine the sugar, water, and wine. Cook over low heat until the sugar is dissolved and the mixture is simmering, stirring constantly. Stand the pears in the pan, cover, and cook for 30 to 35 minutes, or until a knife inserted in the thickest part of the pears pierces them easily, turning the pears occasionally. Remove the pears to a shallow dish and set aside, leaving the liquid in the pan. Increase the heat to medium and cook for 10 to 12 minutes, or until the mixture reaches a syrupy consistency. Pour the syrup over the pears and chill for at least 2 hours, or until ready to serve.

NOTE: It's also great to serve these warm, with a scoop of ice cream and some warm syrup over it all. It makes an unbeatable double treat!

Adults-Only Italian Fruit Salad

8 to 10 servings

This one's strictly for grown-ups—a fruit salad with a kick that's sure to perk up any party!

¾ cup Galliano liqueur (see Note)
½ cup orange juice
1 pineapple, peeled, cored, and cut into 1-inch chunks
3 medium-sized oranges, peeled and cut into 1-inch chunks

2 medium-sized pears, cored and cut into 1-inch chunks
3 medium-sized apples, cored and cut into 1-inch chunks

In a large bowl, combine the liqueur and orange juice. Add the fruit and toss to coat. Cover and chill for at least 3 hours before serving.

NOTE: You can substitute almost any liqueur for the Galliano, but Galliano has its own unique flavor. Prefer an alcohol-free dessert? Use additional orange juice instead of liqueur.

Simple Hazelnut Gelato

about 1½ quarts

It had never occurred to me that making gelato could be so easy. Then I tried this recipe and made it a weekly occurrence.

1 container (8 ounces) frozen whipped topping, thawed
½ cup chocolate-hazelnut spread

1 quart vanilla ice cream, softened

In a large bowl, combine the whipped topping and hazelnut spread until thoroughly mixed. Place the ice cream in a large plastic bowl and stir in the hazelnut mixture until thoroughly combined. Cover tightly and freeze for at least 8 hours, or until firm.

NOTE: For added flavor and crunch, mix in ½ cup toasted chopped hazelnuts with the ice cream . . . or just sprinkle them on top. Crunch, crunch, crunch!

Lemon Ice

about 1½ quarts

If you've ever wanted to stroll down the streets of Italy on a warm summer day, a couple of slurps of lemon ice will practically make you think you're there.

4 cups water
2 cups sugar
1 tablespoon grated lemon peel

1 cup fresh lemon juice (juice of about 6 lemons)
(see Note)

In a large saucepan, bring the water, sugar, and lemon peel to a boil over high heat. Add the lemon juice, reduce the heat to medium, and cook for 5 minutes. Pour into a 2-quart baking dish and let cool to room temperature. Cover and freeze for 2 to 3 hours, or until the liquid has frozen 1 inch in from the sides. Remove from the freezer and mix well, being sure to blend the ice crystals with the remaining liquid. Place in an airtight container, seal, and freeze for 6 to 8 hours, or until firm.

NOTE: *It's really best to use fresh-squeezed lemon juice here. Of course, you may want to strain it first to remove any seeds! Oh— if you like your lemon ice really smooth and creamy, process it in a food processor for 20 to 30 seconds after removing it from the freezer; then refreeze it, as above.*

Tortoni

12 to 14 cups

They'll all scream for this Italian dessert favorite once they find out we know the secret to making it ourselves!

1½ cups frozen whipped topping, thawed
1 quart vanilla ice cream, softened (see Note)
1½ teaspoons almond extract

½ cup plus 2 tablespoons chopped blanched almonds, divided
6 to 7 maraschino cherries, cut in half

Line 12 to 14 muffin cups with paper baking cups. In a large bowl, fold the whipped topping into the ice cream; mix well. Add the almond extract and ½ cup almonds; mix well. Place about ⅓ cup of the ice cream mixture in each muffin cup. Sprinkle with the remaining 2 tablespoons almonds. Cover and freeze for 2 to 3 hours. Just before serving, garnish each with a maraschino cherry half.

NOTE: *To soften the ice cream, place it in a large bowl, break it up, and stir with a wooden spoon.* **Do not let the ice cream reach the melting point.**

Tartufo

12 tartufi

Here's a winning frosty trio—with a cherry surprise in every bite!

½ gallon vanilla ice cream
12 chocolate-covered cherries

1 container (7¼ ounces) chocolate-flavored hard-shell topping

Line a 12-cup muffin tin with paper baking cups and place a scoop of ice cream in each. Push a chocolate-covered cherry into each scoop and top with another rounded scoop of ice cream. If necessary, freeze for 10 minutes to harden the ice cream. Pour an equal amount of hard-shell topping over each rounded mound of ice cream, completely covering the ice cream. Freeze for 1 to 2 hours, or until firm. Serve, or cover and keep frozen until ready to serve.

NOTE: Sure, you can make these with chocolate ice cream or even black cherry ice cream—it's up to you. Any of your favorites should taste great this way!

Cannoli Pie

8 to 10 servings

Better leave room for dessert, 'cause here's a pie version of the classic Italian pastry. Mmm, mmm—I can't get enough of this!

1 container (15 ounces) ricotta cheese
1 cup confectioners' sugar
¼ cup chopped maraschino cherries
¼ cup blanched chopped almonds
¼ cup mini semisweet chocolate chips
One 9-inch chocolate graham cracker pie crust

In a large bowl, stir the ricotta cheese and confectioners' sugar until smooth and well combined. Stir in the cherries, almonds, and chocolate chips. Spoon into the pie crust, cover, and freeze for at least 3 hours. Remove from the freezer and allow to sit for at least 10 to 15 minutes before cutting. Cover and store any leftovers in the freezer.

NOTE: When I want to make this look really fancy, I top each slice with a dollop of whipped topping and a maraschino cherry just before serving.

Index

Mr. Food® Can Help You Be A Kitchen Hero!

Let **Mr. Food**® make your life easier with Quick, No-Fuss Recipes and Helpful Kitchen Tips for

Family Dinners • Soups and Salads • Potluck Dishes • Barbecues • Special Brunches • Unbelievable Desserts

. . . and that's just the beginning!

Complete your **Mr. Food**® cookbook library today. It's so simple to share in all the **"OOH IT'S SO GOOD!!®"**

✂ -

TITLE	PRICE	QUANTITY	
A. **Mr. Food**® Cooks Like Mama	@ $12.95 each	x _____	= $_____
B. The **Mr. Food**® Cookbook, *OOH IT'S SO GOOD!!*®	@ $12.95 each	x _____	= $_____
C. **Mr. Food**® Cooks Chicken	@ $ 9.95 each	x _____	= $_____
D. **Mr. Food**® Cooks Pasta	@ $ 9.95 each	x _____	= $_____
E. **Mr. Food**® Makes Dessert	@ $ 9.95 each	x _____	= $_____
F. **Mr. Food**® Cooks Real American	@ $14.95 each	x _____	= $_____
G. **Mr. Food**®'s Favorite Cookies	@ $11.95 each	x _____	= $_____
H. **Mr. Food**®'s Quick and Easy Side Dishes	@ $11.95 each	x _____	= $_____
I. **Mr. Food**® Grills It All in a Snap	@ $11.95 each	x _____	= $_____
J. **Mr. Food**®'s Fun Kitchen Tips and Shortcuts (and Recipes, Too!)	@ $11.95 each	x _____	= $_____
K. **Mr. Food**®'s Old World Cooking Made Easy	@ $14.95 each	x _____	= $_____
L. "Help, **Mr. Food**®! Company's Coming!"	@ $14.95 each	x _____	= $_____
M. **Mr. Food**® Pizza 1-2-3	@ $12.00 each	x _____	= $_____
N. **Mr. Food**® Meat Around the Table	@ $12.00 each	x _____	= $_____
O. **Mr. Food**® Simply Chocolate	@ $12.00 each	x _____	= $_____
P. **Mr. Food**® A Little Lighter	@ $14.95 each	x _____	= $_____
Q. **Mr. Food**® From My Kitchen to Yours: Stories and Recipes from Home	@ $14.95 each	x _____	= $_____
R. **Mr. Food**® Easy Tex-Mex	@ $11.95 each	x _____	= $_____
S. **Mr. Food**® One Pot, One Meal	@ $11.95 each	x _____	= $_____
T. **Mr. Food**® Cool Cravings: Easy Chilled and Frozen Desserts	@ $11.95 each	x _____	= $_____
U. **Mr. Food**®'s Italian Kitchen	@ $14.95 each	x _____	= $_____
V. **Mr. Food**®'s Simple Southern Favorites	@ $14.95 each	x _____	= $_____

Book Total $_____

+ Postage & Handling for *First Copy*   **4.00**

+ $1 Postage & Handling for Ea. Add'l. Copy
(Canadian Orders Add Add'l. $2.00 *Per Copy*) $_____

$_____

Send payment to:
Mr. Food®
P.O. Box 9227
Coral Springs, FL 33075-9227

Subtotal $_____

Name _____

Street _____ Apt._____

Add 6% Sales Tax
(FL Residents Only) $_____

City _____ State_____ Zip_____

BKU1

Total in U.S. Funds $_____

Method of Payment: ☐ Check or ☐ Money Order Enclosed

Please allow up to 6 weeks for delivery.